To Dad ...... pa
Happ: t
Love   es

Alice + William

and Happy Fishing!

CW01481146

Trout Fishing in New Zealand

Trout Fishing in New Zealand

REX FORRESTER

 **Pacific**

ACKNOWLEDGMENTS

While writing this book I applied to a good many experts and expert fishermen for advice, assistance, facts, figures and know how. For such help I wish to thank, in the first place, those dedicated Wildlife men of the Internal Affairs Department, especially Pat Burstall, Norrie Ewing, Dick Hutchinson, John Gibbs and Trevor Thomson, who put up with my endless questions. Neck and neck with them in second place are all those very capable fishing guides who obligingly wrote to me about their favourite rivers and streams and what to fish them with, especially Fred Gill, Les Wilson, Peter Cullen, Ted Tapper, Lyndsay Taylor, Tony Jensen, Stan and Rea Potts, Bob Sullivan, Simon Dickie, Andy Lennox and Goeff McDonald. Thirdly all those fearless pilots who have flown me into remote places and often had me peering down into promising pools from nought height and at stall speed, especially Tex Smith, Ron Fincham, Bill Black, Goodwin McNutt and Brian Brooker — that's what I call 'fly fishing'! Fourthly all those American visitors who have taught me so much about conservation and sportsmanship and have been such fun to fish with, anglers like Mel Kreiger, Ted Trueblood, Joe King, Tom Collins, Ed Zern, Walt Powell, Warren Petersen and many others. And lastly my wife, who has all too often kept the home hearth warm while I've been away 'enjoying myself' in the name of work, up to my elbows in an icy creek.

To all these and the hundreds more I have fished with, learnt from and swapped the odd lie with, there is only one word on the line—thanks!

Front cover: The author playing a rainbow on beautiful Whakapapa stream with Mt Ruapehu in background. *Photograph by Ralph Anderson*

PACIFIC

Penguin Books (NZ) Ltd, 182–190 Wairau Road, Auckland 10, New Zealand
Penguin Books Ltd, 27 Wrights Lane, London W8 5TZ, England
Viking Penguin Inc., 40 West 23rd Street, New York, New York 10010, USA
Penguin Books Australia Ltd, 487 Maroondah Highway, Ringwood, Australia 3134
Penguin Books Canada Ltd, 2801 John Street, Markham, Ontario, Canada L3R 1B4
Penguin Books Ltd, Registered Offices: Harmondsworth, Middlesex, England

First published by Whitcoulls Publishers, 1979
Reprinted 1979
Revised limp edition, 1987
This edition published by Penguin Books (NZ) Ltd, 1989
Copyright © Rex Forrester, 1979, 1987
10 9 8 7 6 5 4 3 2 1

All rights reserved

Designed by
Printed in Singapore

CONTENTS

Fishing
for
Trout

Trout fishing is the great equaliser, for under its spell all men are equal. A very good friend once remarked, 'If all men were fishermen, there would be no need for psychiatrists.' In my experience anglers form a brotherhood which must be the envy of many secret societies. There are no rules laid down for conduct. Anglers make their own ideals and respect those of others. Anglers are sportsmen and, more important, they are participants. They do not pay professionals to play the sport for them, then sit at home and watch the action on the TV screen; they do it themselves. It's a sport which gives riches in memories to a poor man and can make rich men humble. My favourite cartoon shows a barefoot boy laden down with fish and carrying a homemade rod with cotton reel and line and a bent pin for a hook. Looking on enviously is an angler with the latest equipment but no fish. Several times I have actually seen this scene acted out in real life.

Fishing is a sport that one can share with others, especially with one's children or in family togetherness. The clearest proof of its 'share-value' is the lie-swapping sessions for which anglers are so notorious. In a world where material possessions often count for too much, fishing is also a great equaliser. My favourite uncle put it all in a clamshell one evening when we were sitting in an anchored boat fly fishing at the Awahou stream mouth on Lake Rotorua. 'See that feller over there in that boat,' he said. 'Well, he's the meanest, crookedest and toughest businessman in town, but right now, while he's fishing, there's not a bad thought in his head.'

My own introduction to fishing came early and instilled in me the enthusiasm which is still part of me. I was brought up at Arapuni, south of Cambridge, and besides catching my share of eels in the Waikato River, I regularly played hookey from school to go trolling in canoes and rowboats on Lake Arapuni. However, as those were the days of opportunity I became a professional hunter at the age of fifteen and hunting took hold of me for the next few years. This left little time for fishing, although, like most professional hunters, I did learn the trick of taking the odd trout with a nickel spinner (.303 bullet) when hungry in the mountains.

It wasn't until I was promoted to deer field officer-ranger at Ruatahuna, 110 kilometres east of Rotorua, that I again took up fishing seriously. Since part of my job was to check anglers' licences, survey streams and liberate trout, I thought I should learn how to fish correctly. After all, the Wildlife Service exists primarily to provide good trout fishing for anglers, and a good ranger should know both ends of the business. One day I drove into Rotorua and consulted my uncle, a well known local angler, and told him I needed a complete

(Opposite) Youngsters get a free lesson from an old hand (former guide Tony Jensen) by the Whakapapa Stream, National Park, an upper tributary of the Wanganui River

8

Barry Grouby, 8½-year-old Rotorua fisherman, with the winning trout caught by a junior angler in the Rotorua International Trout-fishing Competition, November 1977. Trout was caught trolling a Cobra lure on Lake Tarawera, weighed 2.66 kg (approx. 6 lb) and had a condition factor of 54

fly-fishing outfit. In the local sports shop he whipped rods and wound reels with a great show of knowledge and professionalism. When I left the shop, I had a new Greenheart rod, fly reel and line, a net, reels of cast, a fly box filled with flies, and an empty wallet. Back to his lawn we went, where he proceeded to give me casting lessons in the old English style, complete with rolled-up newspaper under my right arm. After a couple of hours of hitting myself on the back of the head with rocketing line, I felt reasonably confident.

That night I made the historic announcement to my wife that next day I would proceed to a trout-filled pool on the Whakatane River and return loaded down with a limit bag of fat rainbows. To appreciate that statement you must realise that up until that time I had been working with a bunch of rough, tough, straight-shooting deercullers unique to this country. They feared no man and were a group of individualists known for their self-reliance and the ability to laugh off incredible hardships—a rare breed in this day of automation. I was boss to a bunch of the toughest, and to them angling was for sissies, a gentle art for gentle people.

That evening several of them arrived at my home and on hearing of my proposed fishing trip they broke into uncontrollable laughter. This, they said, they would have to witness. I felt like crawling under the table. However, early next morning saw me leading the 'safari', with my wife just behind (as all good wives should be) and in the rear a raggle-taggle bunch of deerhunters. They were taking great delight in offering advice such as, 'Where's yer gillie, old boy?', 'What about yer pepper and salt hat with all the flies stuck in it?' and 'We should have brought along a truck to bring the fish home in.'

With some apprehension I arrived at a pool which usually held half a dozen good rainbows, and the jocularities continued as I put on a very professional show of assembling the tackle. I wished I was any place but there and was silently cursing myself for opening my big mouth. With the whole group watching my every move, I walked to the head of the pool, paid out a few metres of line and made a mighty back cast. The fly caught in a fuchsia tree and on my forward cast the rod snapped clean in two. I never even got the line in the water. My audience fell to the ground, rolling around in stomach-holding hysteria. I finished up joining them. There must be a moral there somewhere. It was a lesson I shall never forget, and I sincerely hope that others never have such a humbling, mind-shattering introduction to the sport. But one thing is for sure—there's a tremendous camaraderie and a wealth of humour in all things fishing.

There are many ways to fish for trout. One can do it the easy way by spinning, baitcasting or trolling. With a little more skill, one can fish with a wet or dry fly or with a shooting-head line. It doesn't really matter what form of fishing you prefer as long as there is satisfaction and enjoyment in it. It is said that there is a certain amount of snobbery in fishing—fly casters look down on trollers, spin casters are treated with disdain, and dry-fly anglers are a race apart. This is utter rot. I know men who started out as spin fishermen and finished up as dry-fly anglers. One chap who was a dry-fly man now gets his enjoyment by fishing with wire lines. The main thing is that you are fishing.

I do, however, recommend that anyone learning to fish for trout should first learn to fly-fish. Fly-fishing gives the utmost satisfaction, for in learning to use the different flies you will understand more about the trout and why he takes them, and you will get more of a feeling for angling. One of the greatest benefits of becoming a fly angler in New Zealand is that it opens up so many more places for you. In reading through the following pages you will find that many of the best places to fish are designated 'fly only', meaning that you can fish there only with a fly. Everyone enjoys watching a proficient fly caster. I know several men who get their main pleasure from casting—the fish are secondary. Once you have mastered the art, it is then relatively easy to add a spinning rod to your tackle collection. With two strings to your bow, you will often catch fish on one when the other isn't producing.

Trolling has always been referred to as 'lazy man's fishing' because there is not much skill attached to it and anyone should be able to troll whether he is familiar with a rod or not. Well, I admit that it is one of the best forms of relaxation I know, but there is a lot more skill to the sport than you might think. I have spent thousands of hours trolling and have seen unskilled trollers lose three fish out of four, and many times observed only one boat in ten having any success. So don't write it off as unskilled. It is the best form of getting a family or group together, where all have an equal chance of success and everyone becomes involved. So whatever method gives you enjoyment stick with it.

From my hilarious beginnings as an eager young rod snapper, I have progressed through all forms of trout fishing and fished widely throughout New Zealand. I am not an expert, although I have been called one. I am just an average fisherman who has made for himself perhaps more opportunities to fish than many, purely because I like doing it. I fish reasonably well with a wet-fly line and am guilty occasionally of slapping the water with my forward cast. I have caught many a trout on a dry fly, and would like to spend more time at this type of fishing. I own a spinning rod and reel and have been known to toss out a spinner when I thought there were no fly fishermen watching. I have owned several boats, some of which I operated as charter fishing boats, and have spent many happy hours trolling. I can best be described as a typical Kiwi angler—Jack of all trades, master of none. Of the thousands of anglers I have guided, including my family, my greatest satisfaction has been derived from watching the pleasure on people's faces when they have been playing a fighting trout. That, to me, is what my life as hunter, guide and fisherman has been all about.

I have written this book in the hope that you will learn more about the fishing available in this great country of ours, share some of my experiences, and in the following pages hear the sweetest music in the form of a screaming reel, feel the thrill of a bent rod and the lip-biting lunges as a trout battles a tight line.

Tranquil fishing water off the Haast Pass road

Trout Species
in
New Zealand

The pioneering years in this country were busy years. A home and a living had to be carved from a wilderness. As well, there were other things to occupy these pioneers, like goldrushes and the Maori Wars. But even with all this toil and interrupting skirmishes, the anglers among the early settlers began to think about creating a sport fishery. Have you ever noticed that when no leisure time is available an angler always seems to be able to make some? It is surprising the number of busy men one sees out fishing when they should be working.

Our pioneers were no exception. Most were English or Scots and they recognised ideal trout habitat when they saw it in the hundreds of clear, rippling, gravel-bedded streams and gin-clear, sandy-bottomed lakes. Many of the mountain streams had a small native fish in them known to the Maoris as a kokopu (*galaxias*) and often called a native trout, but which rarely exceeded 150 mm in length. The rivers and streams which flowed to the sea had such migratory fishes in them as eels and mullet, scarcely a sport fishery. The food supply for any species they wished to introduce was abundant—freshwater crayfish, snails, smelt and galaxias, insects such as caddis, mayfly, beetles and moths, to name but a few. So with food supply plentiful, water temperature and habitat ideal, they wasted no time in arranging importation of ova of the most popular species from Europe and America. The idea caught on like wildfire and energetic committees sprang up all over the country, which later became known as acclimatisation societies; twenty-three of them are still in existence today. It was these societies, encouraged by men of foresight like T. E. Donne of the Tourist Department, that were responsible for importing, breeding and liberating the forbears of the sport fishery that now enjoys a world-wide reputation.

The 1860s saw the first shipments of ova arrive in New Zealand from the United Kingdom and Tasmania. The early records of importations and liberations are in many cases duplicated or inaccurate, and some confusion does exist. Much arose from the fact that Atlantic salmon, rainbow and brown trout all have the prefix *Salmo* to their Latin identifications. Atlantic salmon are *Salmo salar*, rainbows are *Salmo gairdnerii* and browns are *Salmo trutta*. It would have been very easy for a shipping clerk spotting 'Salmo' on a shipment of rainbow trout ova to put them down as salmon and vice versa. Also in the southern part of the South Island it is still common to hear reference to 'salmon trout', which adds to the confusion.

Early liberations often went astray. A man might set out with good intentions of liberating fry in a given area but en route, through unforseen circumstances, he could be forced to dump them elsewhere. For instance, in researching Tourist Department records I read how Mackinaw or Great Lakes char were liberated in Lake Ianthe in 1906. Further research showed that though these trout were destined for Lake Ianthe in Westland, they never actually reached there but were liberated into Lake Pearson in Canterbury. The reason is not known, but it must be assumed either that the liberation vehicle broke down or the trout started to die on the journey from Christchurch where they were hatched.

This was a common occurrence even in the 1950s when I was working at the Rotorua hatchery, as we were still using a primitive method of transporting fry and fingerlings. The cans had small holes drilled in the top to allow air to circulate when water bubbled up and down through them. There was also a ridge allowing blocks of ice to be placed around the top, which kept the water temperature down. The speed and jolting on rough roads caused the water to be well agitated, thus supplying the trout with plenty of oxygen. This

Modern transportation units for carrying fingerlings to liberation points. Background: Truck unit of the Wildlife Service, Department of Internal Affairs, used for liberations throughout the North Island. Foreground: Trailer pump circulation unit used by the Tauranga Acclimatisation Society

Fingerlings being slowly acclimatised to river water temperature before swimming away to freedom

method was a far cry from the modern tankers of today, which are equipped with temperature-controlled refrigeration equipment and water-circulating pumps. We also made our liberation runs at night when quiet roads allowed for unobstructed speed and the air temperature was at its lowest. We even had blast air horns fitted to warn other vehicles that they were about to be overtaken.

I left Rotorua once with a load of fingerlings destined for the Gisborne district. All went well until I began dropping down the hills into the Bay of Plenty, where I ran into a very warm northerly wind which raised the temperature in the cans alarmingly. I headed for the Opotiki dairy factory, the only place where ice could be obtained, but found it closed. Going on through the Waioeka gorge, the warm wind was now on my tail and the temperature rose even higher. It was obvious my passengers were not going to make Gisborne. There was no alternative but to liberate them in the Waioeka River alongside the road.

The same thing happened to Ray Irvine, who was for many years senior fisheries officer at Rotorua. He was heading for the Hobson district, north of Auckland, with a load of fingerlings and finished up dropping them into Lake Karapiro, near Cambridge, which gave the Auckland Acclimatisation Society an unexpected free bonus that year. In many cases like this, even in the early years, it is certain that to avoid embarrassing explanations unscheduled liberations often went unrecorded. Scotty McGregor, also a senior field officer, once made a liberation that might otherwise have never been made. He was travelling from Rotorua to Hawke's Bay with brown trout fingerlings when the temperature caught up with him on the Kaingaroa Plains. The trout started dying and he began to look desperately for a place to liberate the survivors. In his deerculling days he had hunted around Poronui Station and remembered that there was a small lake named Pourua not far from the main highway, so he turned off and made his liberation.

So even in the 1950s many species were often introduced to places more from expedience than by design. Our pioneers didn't have it all on their own.

My experience of driving hatchery trucks often produced a bonus in unexpected privileges. I was driving with Bill Axbey, former Conservator of Wildlife at Queenstown, one day. We were speeding into Rotorua carrying adult trout from Lake Tarawera to the Rotorua hatchery. As we approached the 50 km/h limit an all-too-familiar siren brought us to a screeching halt. 'Don't stop us now,' said my partner in crime. 'We have live trout aboard and have to keep them moving or they will die.' The officer asked where we were going, then

Maureen Eade of Tuai proudly holds one of the biggest trout taken in New Zealand of recent times — a 12.76 kg (28 lb) brown, which was caught by her brother Rona Lake on a Red Setter fly from Lake Whakamarino in January 1984. The prize catch of the year

with a grim look on his face said, 'Follow me.' To our great delight, he escorted us with siren blaring, at fire-engine speed, through the heart of town. We felt like heroes in a New York ticker-tape parade. My partner's only comment was, 'This bloke must be a fisherman.'

Most liberations involved fish at the fry stage, about 65 days old and 2.5 cm long. They were transported in cans on horseback or dray to almost every corner of the country. In latter years it has proved more successful to liberate fish at the fingerling stage, usually 12 to 14 months old and measuring anything from 10 to 16 cm. They seem to have a much better chance of survival. The first liberations of the following importations are as near as I can establish actual dates from my research, allowing of course for some of the confusion in early records.

BROWN TROUT (*Salmo trutta*)

Brown trout were the first type to be introduced into New Zealand, and were established in the South Island long before the North Island. The South Island was more peaceful in the 1860s, whereas the North Island was a battle ground with General Cameron's campaign against the Waikatos in full swing. Also the Urewera, Rotorua and Taupo regions were in a turmoil as Whitmore and McDonnell chased the Maori renegade Te Kooti. This obviously prevented any peaceful expedition into these regions carrying cans of trout.

Brown trout are a native of Europe where they are found from the British Isles in the west to Russia in the east, and from Spain in the south to Norway in the north. The trout is golden brown in colour turning to yellow on the belly, although long periods in a river will often turn the golden brown to black. The top half of the body is covered with blacks spots and along the lateral line are red to gold spots of the same size. The tail is square with few or no spots. They prefer to spawn in gravel-bottomed streams, but will spawn in lakes along shallow rocky or sandy foreshore areas. Spawning takes place in the winter months, mainly from May to July.

The average size of browns in lakes is 1.3 to 1.8 kg, though in rivers that run to the sea the average is lower at 0.9 to 1.3 kg. Where browns run to the sea, as in South Westland, they often return an average around 2.2 kg and are silver in colour. In this condition in South Westland they are often referred to as 'salmon trout'.

Browns were first shipped from England to Tasmania in the early 1860s, and the first report of their being transferred to New Zealand states that a Mr Johnson of Christchurch imported the first successful ova from Hobart in 1867, which formed the initial basis of Canterbury

Three typical rainbows taken by the author at the Tongariro River delta in 1975. Top: Jack, 2 kg (4½ lb). Middle: Hen, 2.4 kg (5¼ lb). Bottom: Hen, 1.3 kg (2¾ lb).

stock.[1] However, George Ferris in his book *Fly Fishing in New Zealand* (1954) states that these attempts in 1867 were unsuccessful. He reports the first successful shipment as being brought to Otago in 1868 by a Mr Clifford, curator of the Otago Acclimatisation Society, and that the number of ova imported was 800. It is interesting to note that both authorities give the same number of ova, which often compounds the confusion of early records. So it can be taken that by 1868 brown trout were established in this country. It is worth noting

[1] G. M. Thomson, *The Naturalisation of Animals and Plants in New Zealand*, Cambridge, 1972.

22

too that liberations of Brown trout into the U.S.A. did not take place until 1883, fifteen years after their introduction to New Zealand. It was not until 1886 that they found their way into Lake Taupo in the North Island.[2]

The first recorded taking of a brown trout on rod and line was in the Water of Leith, Dunedin, on opening day of the 1874 season, the angler being a Mr A. C. Begg.[3]

Present distribution. Most streams, rivers and lakes throughout both islands of New Zealand. There are, however, many lakes without browns.

RAINBOW TROUT *(Salmo gairdnerii)*

The rainbow trout is a native of North America where it is more predominant in the northwest. It is the most sought-after trout in the world because of its renowned fighting qualities. Rainbows that spawn in rivers that flow to the sea and actually live at sea for periods of their lives are known as 'Steelheads'. This is because of their colouring. The sides of the body, and especially the head, have a brilliant freshly minted chromium or steel-like sheen, which gives them their name. In North America rainbows that are land-locked in lakes are sometimes known as 'Kamloops trout'.

The majority of rainbows in New Zealand have a similar life pattern to steelheads, in that lakes are their 'sea' for most of the year and they run up tributary streams and rivers to spawn. The fish is a steel-green along the back, turning silver along the belly. The back is heavily covered with brown or black spots. It is pink to red along the lateral line from which it derives its name and this red colouring becomes inflamed during spawning, turning often to a vivid red on the gill covers. The tail is square and heavily spotted. Rainbows fresh run from the sea or taken deep in inland lakes are brilliant silver in colour with only a faint pink flush. When spawning they turn much darker, often black, even along the belly. The average weight of this fish in New Zealand is 0.9 to 1.4 kg, but there are exceptions. For instance, in Lake Taupo they have been averaging 2.0 kg (4½ lb) for many years due to sound fishery management. In Lake Tarawera, the country's glamour rainbow lake, the average is 2.3 kg (5 lb).

Spawning runs take place from as early as March until as late as November, and summer runs are not uncommon. But the main spawning runs take place from July to October. Rainbows prefer clear

[2] O. S. Hintz, *Trout at Taupo*, London, 1955.
[3] G. J. Benfield, *Trout and Salmon Fishing in Otago . . .*, Dunedin, 1948.

gravel-bottomed streams, but will spawn along the shallow, rocky or sandy foreshores of lakes. The average female lays up to 2500 eggs in a shallow depression or redd, which she hollows out in the stream bed. In making a redd she will lie on her side wriggling her body energetically and moving her tail from side to side until a depression is formed in the sand and gravel. Here she deposits her eggs and the male trout, or 'jack' as he is commonly called, will move up and fertilise the eggs with his milt, a milk-like fluid. Repeated fresh runs of trout will dig new redds over old ones, destroying them and washing out eggs laid by previous females. These eggs will drift downstream, often to be cannibalised by other trout which follow the spawning fish for this purpose. It has been estimated that only one per cent of ova will reach maturity.

It was in 1883 that New Zealand received its first shipment of rainbow ova from the United States, ironically the year that that country imported its first shipment of brown trout ova from Europe. An earlier shipment was landed in New Zealand in 1878 but it is not known for certain whether it was of rainbows or cut-throats, so the 1883 shipment must be taken as the first acceptable importation of rainbow trout.

It had always been believed that a man named La Motte shipped or stripped the ova and that they came from the Russian River at a place called Guerneville, about 110 kilometres north of San Francisco. In 1960 Mr P. J. Burstall, the Conservator of Wild Life at Rotorua and one of this country's foremost authorities on trout, visited the Guerneville site but considered it to be a staging-point. It was then discovered that La Motte had operated a hatchery at Gibson Creek near the Russian River at Ukiah. Consequently it was suggested that the ova could have come from Gibson Creek and been held at Guerneville awaiting a ship leaving San Francisco for New Zealand.

However, when I was In California in 1976 several local anglers drew my attention to the research work being carried out into the origins of the New Zealand rainbow. Working jointly on the project were Mr J. C. Fraser, regional manager of the California Fish and Game Department at Yountville, California, Dr D. Scott of the University of Otago, New Zealand, and Mr John Hewitson of Encinitas, California. Their considerable research shows that the 1883 shipment came from the steelhead run of rainbows in Sonoma Creek, California. I quote from Mr Fraser's letter to me of 6 April 1977:

A. V. La Motte, whose name was associated with the 1883 shipment in the New Zealand records, had operated a fish hatchery on Gibson Creek, near the Russian River at Ukiah. I am confident this fact gave rise to the mistaken belief that the 1883 eggs came from the Russian River. However, La Motte did not start to operate the

Gibson Creek hatchery until 1897. Actually the 1883 eggs came from Sonoma Creek, a stream directly tributary to San Francisco Bay where the same A. V. La Motte operated a fish hatchery from 1878 to at least 1890. I am convinced that the chances of the 1883 eggs having come from the Russian River are negligible. It is equally unlikely that they were shipped to Guerneville. There is no real evidence of Guerneville being involved. The 1883 eggs were most likely shipped directly by train and boat from Sonoma to San Francisco where they were transferred to the ship embarking for New Zealand. Sonoma Creek steelheads were, with little doubt, the origin of the 1883 eggs.

This ova was raised successfully in ponds in the Auckland domain, whence the species was eventually liberated throughout the entire country.

Present distribution: Most rivers, streams and lakes throughout both islands. Liberations have been made in the remotest areas to which ova and fry could be carried by back pack and on horseback, and fingerlings have been dropped into remote lakes from aircraft.

BROOK TROUT *(Salvelinus fontinalis)*

This fish is not actually a trout but, like the Mackinaw or lake trout, is a member of the char family and is a native of the northeastern part of the North American continent. It is a golden-coloured fish, although in New Zealand its colouring it is not unlike that of the rainbow, except for its distinguishing marks. These are red spots along the lateral line, each surrounded by a ring with a bluish tinge. Other features are the white leading edge of each of its lower fins, and the dark wavy lines along its back and dorsal fin. It is an excellent sporting fish, renowned for its tenacious fighting qualities. In New Zealand wherever it has been released in direct competition with other species such as rainbow and brown trout it has not fared well, and because both are so widespread the brook trout's range is extremely limited. However, where it has the water to itself, as in Lake Emily in the Canterbury high country and in the Hinemaiaia Dam near Taupo, the average weight is 0.9 to 1.3 kg, although bigger fish have been taken. In much of its habitat, such as small farm streams and drains, the average mature fish measures around 152 mm.

A Mr A. M. Johnson is given credit for importing the first shipment of brook trout ova from New York via San Francisco in 1887.

Present distribution: North Island—the Hinemaiaia Dam and the Rotorua and Waiouru districts. South Island—Lake Emily and small streams like the Sutton near Middlemarch.

MACKINAW TROUT *(Salvelinus namaycush)*

Like the brook trout, the Mackinaw is a member of the char family, and in its native habitat in North America is known as a lake trout. It is a cold-water fish found from the Great Lakes north to the Arctic Circle and from Alaska in the west to Nova Scotia in the east. It can vary in colour from blue grey to brown and is covered with whitish spots, often of irregular shape, so that the dark areas between the spots give a similar wavy line appearance to that of brook trout. The tail is slightly forked. In its native habitat it prefers living at deep levels. It is often taken at extreme depths up to 60 metres. It prefers to spawn on bouldery lake beds at varying depths up to 30 metres and does not make a redd.

A Mr L. F. Ayson, Chief Inspector of Fisheries, is credited with importing this species in 1906 at the request of the Government Tourist Department. The ova were hatched at the local society's Christchurch hatchery and subsequently released in Lake Pearson, Canterbury. It has not survived well in New Zealand, mainly because it was liberated in the wrong type of water. Possibly it would have done well in glacial lakes like Pukaki and Tekapo, and glacial rivers on the West Coast, like the Fox, Cook and Arawata.

Present distribution: Believed to be only in Lake Pearson, Canterbury, where in 1969 three were reported taken averaging around 0.5 kg (1 lb).

QUINNAT SALMON *(Onchorhynchus tschawytcha)*

The quinnat is a native of the North American continent where it is known as the chinook or king salmon. On the Pacific coast it is found from California in the south to Alaska in the north. During migratory runs in the Yukon, chinooks have been known to travel 3200 kilometres from the sea. In New Zealand this fish is referred to as a Pacific salmon. It is silver in colour, turning to green along the back, which is covered with brown or black spots. In appearance it is not unlike a sea-run or a deep-water rainbow, as its tail is also square. Those caught in New Zealand on coming in from the sea average 2.3 to 6.4 kg (5-14 lb) and in some years have been taken up to 22 kg and more. This is not very different from the weights in the American northwest where they average around 6 to 8 kg, with the largest over 27 kg. The comparison also shows how well the salmon have adapted to a New Zealand habitat. This fish is different from the other main species, Atlantic salmon, rainbow and brown trout, in that it spawns only on returning from the sea. Having spawned, it soon dies, to be washed downstream and out on to gravel banks. The young leave the

Brown trout 2.7 kg (6 lb), taken by Peter Barrett, outdoors editor of True Adventure *magazine, New York, at the Tongariro delta*

streams and migrate to sea as yearlings, returning in March or April as three to four year-olds. The spawning runs are triggered by freshes or floods in the rivers. The female hollows out a redd and spawns in the same manner as rainbow trout.

The first shipments of ova arrived in New Zealand from North America at Auckland in 1875, with a further shipment following in 1876. These were followed by further irregular consignments right up to 1908. The first recorded catch was a female weighing 7.3 kg (16 lb), taken in the Waitaki River in 1906.

Present distribution: The East Coast rivers of the South Island, principally the Waiau, Waimakariri, Rakaia, Ashburton, Rangitata and Waitaki. They are also present in some West Coast rivers of the South Island flowing out of Lakes Paringa and Moeraki and the Okarito Lagoon, although I am told that dead salmon have been found in most rivers from Greymouth south. Landlocked quinnat are much smaller, averaging around 0.9 kg (2 lb), and are found in Lakes Wakatipu, Wanaka, Hawea, Te Anau, Manapouri, Ianthe and Mapourika.

ATLANTIC SALMON *(Salmo salar)*

As its name implies, this is a native of the Atlantic and is to be found on both sides, in both European and American waters. In the west it is found from Boston in the south to Greenland in the north, and in the east from as far south as Portugal to Norway in the north. It is a fish that can easily be confused with brown trout, especially when juvenile, as the colouring is similar. It is blue-black on the back, which is covered with irregular dark spots, and the belly and sides are silver. However, when in a stream they turn much darker, usually a yellow-brown, which is where the confusion with brown trout occurs. The tail is square except in juveniles, when it has a pronounced fork. The protuberance on the lower jaw of the male is more noticeable than in either rainbow or brown trout.

The first shipment of these fish arrived in New Zealand in 1868 and came from the rivers Tay and Severn in Britain. The consignment numbered 100,000 ova. G. J. Benfield states that Mr F. Ayson, Chief Inspector of Fisheries, imported large numbers of these fish in 1908 from Scotland, Ireland, Wales and the Rhine, and that 447,000 were eventually liberated in the Upukerora River at Te Anau. This sounds like an awful lot of fry for one river, so no doubt other streams were also used as liberation points.

Present distribution: Lakes Gunn and Fergus in the Eglington Valley hold the biggest population of these fish in New Zealand and the

Southern Hemisphere. Atlantics caught here have weighed up to 2.3 kg (5 lb) and occasionally up to 3.6 kg (8 lb) They are also landlocked in Lakes Manapouri and Te Anau and several are caught each year between the two lakes. The average weight of these fish is about 0.9 kg (2 lb) and it is interesting to note that where this species has become landlocked in the U.S.A. the average weight also drops to around 0.9 kg.

The Wildlife Service of the Department of Internal Affairs has instigated a management plan for the fish in Lake Gunn and it is hoped eventually to propagate this species in other parts of New Zealand.

CONCLUSION

Of the six imported species known to exist in New Zealand, only the rainbow and brown trout have surpassed all expectations. Indeed, the pioneers responsible for the early liberations of these two species would be justly proud if they could see the results of their foresight and energy—a rainbow and brown trout fishery now revered and renowned throughout the world.

The third most successful immigrant is the quinnat salmon, although its acclimatisation has been limited because the spawning water available has been reduced through the building of hydro dams. In recent years foreign deep-sea trawlers and seiners have reduced the population out at sea before salmon can reach the river mouths. Despite these hurdles, the fishery is holding its own.

Running fourth in the popularity stakes is the brook trout. Its habitat is limited, although there are large stocks available for rehabilitation. For instance, in the 1950s the Wildlife Service took mature brook trout measuring from 101 to 152 mm from a small stream alongside the Taupo road at Rotorua and successfully established them in the virgin waters of the newly built Hinemaiaia Dam. The results were startling, as a few years later, under a special licence, anglers were taking brooks there up to 2.3 kg (5 lb) in weight. This shows how well this trout can prosper with no competition. So although virgin water is limited, this trout could be repopulated successfully if new hydro dams are built.

Similarly, the ailing Atlantic salmon and Mackinaw trout could be revitalised as the smaller acclimatisation societies come under a more centralised controlling body and more finance becomes available for research into their problems. I for one am extremely thankful that with all the trial, experimentation and error that went on in the early years, five of the original imported immigrants have fared so well.

Fly
Fishing

This country was made for fly anglers. In fact, most of the fishing laws were made by fly anglers long before such a thing as spinning tackle was invented. When the fishing season is open, one can fly-fish anywhere, as fly fishermen are not restricted to certain areas like trollers or spinners.

This is the reason I recommend that anyone learning to fish for trout should learn to fly cast—there is so much more water available. To make the most of this, it is advisable to be proficient with both wet and dry fly. A simple rule of thumb to determine the method of fishing is that rivers and streams that flow to the sea have resident populations of trout all year round. These are fished with dry fly or nymph and on some rivers the small English pattern of true wet fly, streamer flies, can be used. On rivers and streams which flow into lakes where the main trout population is migratory they are mainly caught with the lure or streamer fly fished deep. There are exceptions in both cases, but this is a good way of establishing the most popular method.

DRY-FLY FISHING

A dry fly is made to imitate a natural fly floating on the water with tiny wings and limbs. The art of dry-fly fishing is to ascertain what natural flies the trout are rising to and imitate them artificially to fool the trout. Many anglers on reaching a favourite pool will sit and watch a hatch of insects hovering above the water before selecting a similar imitation fly to use. Many examine the stomach contents of the first fish caught to determine what it has been eating.

Fishing with a dry fly calls for a special technique. The angler approaches a pool from below and casts his fly upstream so that it will float down with the current into the vision of the trout, which is lying facing upstream. A floating line is used and the fly is dipped in a solution of dope to prevent it from sinking. With this method the angler will see the fish take the fly, so he should watch the fly carefully and be ready to strike the moment the fish takes it. To repeat, it is always advisable to approach a pool from down stream, as the trout are less likely to spot you. If they do, they will dart about the pool and will seldom take a fly after becoming disturbed. For the same reason, when casting upstream it is essential to false cast and not allow the line to slap the water, as this too will disturb the fish. When fishing a dry fly or nymph, control of the line with the line hand is most important. Take up the slack line with it, making sure there is no belly in the line, but do not pull the line as the fly will not float naturally. A little practice will have a fairly tight line almost up to

General Selection of New Zealand Dry Flies

(from left to right)

Kakahi Queen	Black Ngat	Wickham's Fancy	Coachman	Royal Coachman
Love's Lure	Pope's Nondescript	Butcher	Twilight Beauty	Blue Dunn
Dad's Favourite	Red Spinner Lysaght	Hardy's Favourite	Stone Fly	Pev O Peak
Heckham's Peckham	Grouse and Purple	Palmer Red	G'Wells Woodcock	Waipahe Black
Black Spider	Red Spinner Dark	Alexandra	G'Wells Dark	Waipahe Red
Hare's Ear	Coch-y-Bondhu	Red Tipped Governor	March Brwon Std	March Brwon Purple
Green Beetle	Greenwell's Light	Tupp's Indispensable	Pomohaka Black	March Brwon Male
Brown Beetle	Coch-y-Bondhu Quill	Molefly	Pomohaka Red	March Brwon Female

Selection of Weighted Nymphs

Copper and Hare

Hare's Ear

Olive Nymph

Pheasant Tail

Hunchback Brown

Hunchback Olive

Gold Ribbed Hare's Ear

Riffle Dragon

Troth Leech

Helgramite Larva

Brown Drake

Green Dragon

Muddler Minnows & Matuka Muddlers

Muddler Minnow

Matuka Muddler

Gold Body

Orange Body

Deer Hair Mouse

the fly, so that when the fish bites, one can strike quickly. Slack line results in missed strikes. The spare line can either be coiled in the line hand or dropped at the feet on the water or grass, ready for the next cast. Long-distance casting is seldom required with a dry fly. Most anglers use only 9-15 metres (30-50 ft) of line.

I remember from my deerculling days that blowflies were plentiful

Rod Squires of Sydney with two 4.5 kg (10 lb) rainbows taken on the fly at Lake Tarawera in June 1976

33

*Angler playing a
fighting rainbow at the
Poutu River outlet of
Lake Rotoaira*

around drying deerskins and I used to catch them and feed them to hungry bush-stream trout. Dead flies would often float right through a pool without being eaten, but if I removed a wing from the fly and left it alive, it would seldom make it through the pool. Trout obviously prefer live food. Wounded flies will struggle on the surface and usually try to swim against or across the current. I was to remember this lesson in later years when I took up fishing with a dry fly, and have successfully caught trout by casting across the stream and giving the fly a spurt now and again, trying to make it look alive. However, one has to be very gentle with the line on these occasions or it will alert the fish. So experimentation can bring many happy hours with any method.

A few years back I was fishing the Tongariro River with Ted Trueblood, then fishing editor of *Field and Stream* magazine, and Peter Barrett, outdoors editor of *True Adventure* magazine. We had experienced some excellent fishing on streamer flies fished deep, and because they were first-class anglers who could adapt to local conditions, I told them about the big browns in the lower Tongariro and whetted their appetite. We drove to the lower end of the river, walked to the bank and looked down on three of the biggest browns I had ever seen. They were lying just below the surface in slack water for all the world like waiting submarines. Ted was dying for a chance at them, so we watched while he tried nymphs, dry flies, wet flies, sinking-tip line and floating line—all to no avail. Then Pete and I had a go and, between us, threw the book at them, spooking a dozen or more before we gave up in disgust.

Author's three favourite fly rods. Top: Orvis S.S.S. cane with two tips, length 2.67 m (8' 9"), weight 195 g (6⅞oz), fitted with Orvis magnalite multiplier reel and no. 10 WF line. Middle: Walton Powell fibreglass with fighting butt, length 2.75 m (9'), fitted with Cortland 444 reel and no. 10 high-D line. Bottom: Fenwick FF 9010 fibreglass, length 2.75 m (9'), weight 142 g (5 oz), fitted with Walker Brampton single-action fly reel and no. 10 high-D shooting-head line

That night I phoned Geoff Sanderson, the veteran fishing guide in the area, and asked his advice. He wouldn't give any but would rather show us, and offered to take us out then and there, as it was a perfect black night with no moon. We boated across to the river mouth and felt our way into the shallows. In the light of a torch Geoff produced his own brown trout flies. He tied them from deer hair in a round ball with a long tail, the closest thing to an imitation mouse. He attached these to floating lines and advised the Americans to cast across the river mouth so that the fly would bob down with the current under the overhanging willows. The fly also needed some action to make it look lifelike, which is easier said than done when one is fishing blind.

The results were startling. The stillness of the night was soon shattered by the scream of a reel as Peter battled a 3-kg (7-lb) brown. His face was all smiles as he brought this beauty into the circle of torchlight. We had discovered the Sanderson secret of the Tongariro browns, though we caught some fish and lost others in the difficult conditions. The experience proved to me that there is always someone somewhere who knows the intricacies of fishing familiar water.

NYMPHING

Fishing with nymphs is an exciting variation of dry-fly fishing and probably one of the most deadly methods of trout fishing as well as

The four types of fly used in New Zealand

the hardest. A nymph is the larval stage of aquatic insects such as mayflies, stoneflies, dragonflies, caddis flies, Dobson flies and lacewings. It rises from the stream bed to the surface, where it hatches into a fly or insect to complete its life cycle. They are a favourite food of trout, particularly when rising to the surface.

This method of fishing can be most rewarding, especially if trout are not rising to a dry fly. Artificial nymphs sink, so that they can be fished with a floating line on shallow streams, a slow-sinking line on deeper streams, or a sink-tip line, which I feel is the best of the three. A sink-tip line allows the nymph to sink to the bottom and then, as the line is drawn in by hand, rise towards the surface at an angle in a perfect imitation of the real thing. Unlike dry-fly fishing, where you can watch the fly, you cannot watch the nymph or see the strike. Perfect control and feel of the line is most important as trout take nymphs very softly. One must be ready to strike at any hesitation or pause in the line, no matter how slight. Many anglers use a dry fly tied ahead of the nymph, so that they can watch the fly's progress and strike when it stops or pauses. Nymphs can be fished upstream or down, although the most successful method is usually fishing upstream to the head of the pool. They are very successful on streams with populations of resident trout where insect larvae are a staple diet. On most spawning streams nymphs work when trout are not interested in streamer flies.

WET AND STREAMER-FLY FISHING

The term 'wet fly' is a misnomer; it does not represent a fly at all but is an imitation of a small fish. The tail feather is often long enough to appear to swim and look like the tail of a fish as it is drawn through the water. The small English pattern flies are made to represent aquatic insects or small fish; the larger lure or streamer flies to resemble smelt or bullies, popular forage fish of the trout. Where a dry fly is fished upstream, a wet fly is fished downstream and drawn back towards the angler. The line is retrieved by hand, and the angler can control the speed of the retrieve to simulate the smelt swimming in the water.

The angler should have full control of the line and fly. Although he seldom sees a trout strike, he can set the hook more easily than when dry-fly fishing, because he always has a tight line and can feel the moment a trout strikes. This is the advantage over most other methods of fly fishing.

Wet-fly fishing is most popular on lakes or on rivers and streams

(Opposite) Fishing guide Roger Forrester with happy Australian couple Donna and Tom Courtney of NSW with morning's catch from Lake Tarawera

(Overleaf) Steve Rajeff of San Francisco throws a long loop on the Tongariro River, showing the style which won him the world champion fly-casting title in 1975

when spawning runs are taking place. With its many variations, it is the most popular method of fly fishing in New Zealand. Although it is easier than other methods it does require the ability to cast a fly long distances. Many lake-fishing anglers allow their line to land on the water so as to get more purchase for a longer throw on the next cast. This is known as 'thrashing the water' or 'bullock driving'; it is a common practice. In dry-fly fishing it is *verboten*. Lake trout are not so scary, but it is a practice which should be avoided. False casting on lakes will improve the catch ratio. Successful wet-fly anglers cast an average of 20 metres (70 ft) of line, many can put out the entire 25 metres (90 ft) to the backing, and I know several who regularly cast 30 metres (100 ft), using the double-haul method.

THE RETRIEVE FOR WET-FLY FISHING

In dry-fly fishing the line hand is most important in taking up the slack, whereas in wet-fly fishing the line hand retrieves the line, so controlling the speed of the fly. The retrieve is most important. Once the fly has been cast out, the line hand starts the retrieve to make the fly swim in a lifelike manner. The line hand can either strip in the line and allow it to fall at the angler's feet, whether he is standing in water or a boat, or loop it in coils from the line hand, or coil it just in the palm. The first method is used with either a floating line, which can be picked up easily from the water in the next cast, or with wet or dry line when fishing from a boat. A wet-sinking line should not be dropped on the water as it will sink and be too hard to pick up for the next cast. Coiling or palming the line is probably a better method and should take more fish. To coil the line, the hand holding the rod clasps the line lightly to the rod with the forefinger; the other hand then pulls the line from this finger in short even drags from 10 to 15 centimetres (4 to 6 in.) at a time, sometimes up to 30 centimetres (1 ft) at a time. The line hand coils this line in ever diminishing loops, allowing them to hang from the fingers. The diminishing coils prevent the line from tangling during the next cast. To palm the line, the line can either be taken from the forefinger of the rod-holding hand as in the previous example, or taken directly from the first line guide on the rod. The line hand gets a wrist motion going so that the line is zigzagged across the palm, with the zigzag coils being held in

(Opposite) Author with a brown trout (2.3 kg–5 lb) taken on a fly at the mouth of the Ngongotaha Stream, Lake Rotorua

the palm by the fingers. This palming method is one of the most successful at imitating smelt in the water, mainly, I feel, because the wrist motion only brings the line in from 7 to 10 centimetres (3 to 4 in.) at a time. The speed of the fly can also be greatly varied by either a fast or slow wrist action.

42

Graham Cates

Trolling

Trolling is the second most popular method of fishing for trout in New Zealand. The growth of this sport has been most spectacular in recent years, probably stemming from the increased popularity of pleasure boating. It is an excellent means of relaxation, and not only does it attract new anglers to the sport but it involves whole families in togetherness. Many anglers have their first taste of fishing in this manner and, thus encouraged, move on to other methods. It is an unselfish method of fishing; everyone stands an equal chance—even mother-in-law. It's relaxing, technical, enjoyable and a great equaliser.

Trolling is defined as towing any kind of line behind a boat with a spoon, spinner or wobbler attached for bait. 'Harling' is a term dreamed up by pioneer fly fishermen who didn't want other fly fishermen to know they had been trolling. It means to tow a *fly line* behind a boat with a *streamer fly* attached for bait. However, trolling a fly, even on a lead line, is referred to as harling these days. It's a misnomer, for whatever the bait on any kind of line it's still suspiciously like trolling to me.

As a rule, one trolls a fly as slowly as the boat will go, and the same applies to many forms of wobblers. Spoons and spinners can be trolled a little bit faster.

All types of bait can be trolled successfully in shallow lakes using normal fly lines or lines of monofilament. To get down deeper, lead-core lines are now very popular as they have largely replaced the need to attach weights to the line. For even greater depths, wire lines are used.

Trolling can be accomplished from any form of canoe, rowboat, cabin cruiser, launch or sailboat. Like my sons, I started in both canoe and rowboat. They provide one of the best means of trolling a fly, mainly, I feel, because the stroke of oar or paddle tows the fly through the water in spurts closely imitating the real thing. My only advice for anyone fishing from arm-powered boats is to travel into wind or against the current on the outward journey. Then when you turn for home with arms a lot weaker than when you started, you will have the advantage of wind and current to help you along. Affluence, however, has turned most of us to motor propulsion, and it is rare these days to see anyone trolling by paddle.

Speed with motors is most important. I have owned boats that were not good fish catchers, for even at their slowest idling speed they were still too fast. The wind and type of line used are two factors that will influence speed. Heading into wind will usually restrict and often vary speed, and because of this far more trout are caught trolling into wind than running with it. Again, the drag from, say, two 100-metre lead-core lines will slow the boat down far more than two fly lines of the same length. It is also most difficult to get many large engines to troll slowly enough, for with long periods of slow running one invariably fouls the plugs. With such motors, it is common practice to throw a bucket over the stern on a length of rope, which acts as a sea anchor and reduces speed. Outboard motors up to 20 kW (25 hp) are ideal for trolling, but more powerful motors can bring problems at the idle, depending on the weight of the boat they are pushing. The perfect set-up is to have a large motor for travelling to locations, and a small 1·5-4 kW (2-5 hp) auxiliary outboard for the actual trolling, which also provides the added benefit of safety.

To judge speed correctly with hardware lures, it is always a good idea to pay out about two or three metres of line and hold the rod out to the side of the boat so one can watch the action of the lure. Go too fast and it may spin; too slow and it may not swim correctly. It is not

Author's three favourite trolling reels. Top: English 'Paramount' single-action reel with lead line; fitted to old fly rod. Middle: Penn 85 star drag reel with monofilament line; fitted to old fly rod. Bottom: New Zealand-made 'Stearns' fly reel with fly line; fitted to old spinning-fly combination rod

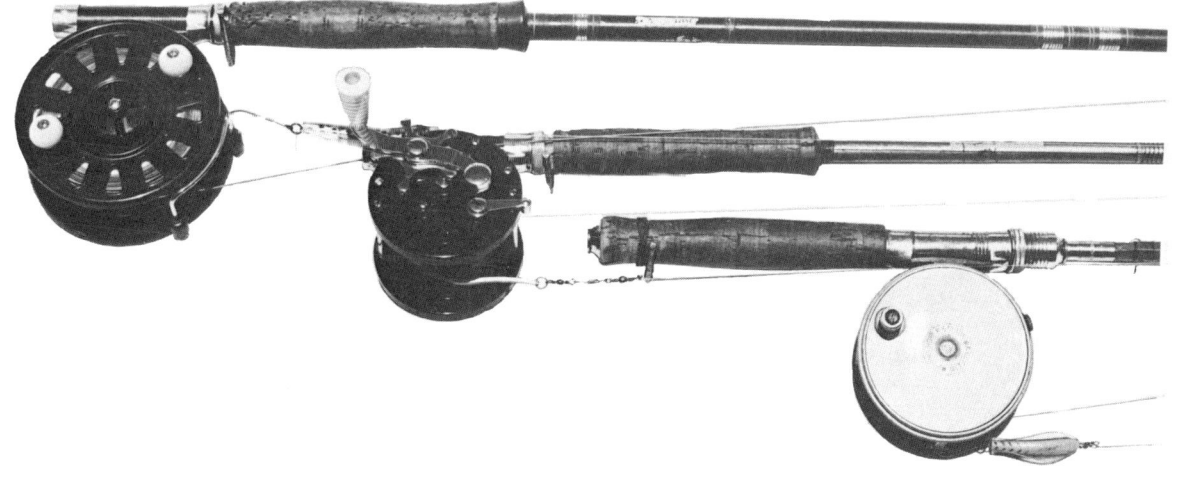

Simon Dickie's floating lodge Waianiwa in trout-hunting mood on Lake Taupo, with the mountains Ruapehu and Tongariro in the background

too difficult to adjust the speed of the boat until the lure is swimming as the maker intended.

Spinners and spoons represent small food fish swimming in a straight line. Trout will often follow these for long distances without striking, and a change in speed will excite the fish into making an attack. It pays to alter speed occasionally, as I have had strikes immediately after either slowing or advancing the throttle. Wobblers have a zigzag motion; they are meant to represent either wounded fish or the action of such things as crayfish and frogs. By watching the action alongside the boat, I have found that they swim most enticingly at the slowest speeds. Altogether, with the correct speed depending on wind, motor, weight of line and type of lure, it becomes very much a matter of trial and error and simple experimentation.

Popular Selection of New Zealand Streamer (Lure) Flies

(from left to right)

Claret and Mallard	Kilwell No. 2	Keeler
Kilwell No. 1	Tamati	Hairy Dog
Ewe Wasp	Ginger Mick	Hamill's Killer
Warden's Worry	Mrs Simpson	Parson's Glory
Black Rabbit	Jack Sprat	Red Setter
Yellow Rabbit	Matuka	Hopes
Leslie's Lure	Dorothy Red	Dappled Dog

Yolanta Green (Australian TV star) showing two typical rainbows caught from the Waianiwa, Lake Taupo

Australian visitors playing large rainbow from Roger Forrester's guide boat on Lake Tarawera, famous for its double-figure rainbows

Similarly, the question of how much line to put out depends on a great many factors such as weight of line, weight of lure, and whether one wishes to troll the lure near the surface or near the bottom. With light fly and monofilament lines with fly attached to either, the trolling will be near the surface, so in this instance I like to pay out at least a hundred metres. I have had far more success with long lines than with short ones. The main advantage with a long line is that though the boat may frighten fish as it passes over or near them, by the time it has travelled a hundred metres or so they should be back on their feeding pattern. However, using the same lines with hardware lures means the lures will run deeper, so a shorter line is needed to fish shallow, but longer to fish deep.

Lead-core lines are for deep fishing. They are made with a different colour for every ten yards (9 m) of line. Theoretically, each colour represents so many metres that the line will sink, so that ten colours, 100 yards (91 m) will be down to 60 feet (18 m) in depth. In practice, however, this depends entirely on the speed of the boat and the type of lure used. The different colours are an excellent guide, though, in remembering how much line you had out when you caught the last fish. It is common to hear trollers remark that they were fishing with five colours or eight, as the case may be. The only sure way of knowing at what depth your lure is fishing is by using a depth-finder. For instance, if you pass over a reef which records at 15 metres and your lure gets hooked up on it, then you know you are down that far. You can then wind in a little line and pass over the same reef again. If you don't get hooked a second time, you can carry on fishing the contours of the lake by following them on the depth-finder at the 15-metre level.

There is no law against the number of lines that can be trolled behind a boat, except that one angler cannot run more than one line. If there is more than one fisherman in the boat, each must hold his own rod in his hand; he cannot place it in a rod-holder.

Common sense applies when it comes to running a number of lines. Two lines from the average small boat, one out to each side, is the ideal set-up. These can be two deep lines or two shallow lines, or one of each. The two rods should be held at right angles out to either side, and kept that way especially during turns, to avoid crossing the lines. A third line can then be run out the stern and pointed straight down the wake. This third line is generally of a different type, again to avoid tangles. This gives a number of combinations such as two lead and one of nylon, two fly and one of nylon, or two fly and one of lead, and so on. It is a good practice in a new area to run three different lines such as nylon, lead and fly, all fishing at different

Rod Bellerby studies a day's bag taken in company with the author from Rod's launch Mako *in Western Bay, Taupo. The fish were caught to order for a travel convention dinner*

depths until you strike oil on one of them. Trolling four lines requires a great amount of care even from the largest launches, otherwise tangles and twisted line will take up a great amount of your fishing time. Charter launches regularly run four lines, but the skipper watches his clients like a hawk and makes them keep their rods in set positions. The waving of any rod through a 45-degree angle will inevitably cause a tangle. A short line of 6-10 metres trolled just at the end of the propeller bubbles often produces surprising results.

50

THE STRIKE AND BOATING THE TROUT

When trolling, there is little need to set the hook. The first warning one gets of a strike is when the trout takes off with the lure like greased lightning, leaving you holding a bent rod and a screaming reel. Trout have a very soft mouth, and an attempt to strike at this moment means that hook and trout will invariably part company. I have seen excitable types—and others—put their back into it and strike hard enough to set the hook in a killer whale. Best thing to do in such a situation is duck, for the spoon will often bounce back and wrap itself around the motor, mast, or some innocent bloke's ear.

The trout will hook itself—there is no need for elaborate flourishes. Once the fish has struck, immediately put the motor into neutral or switch it off and then play the fish as though you were on shore. Other anglers in the boat should wind in their lines to avoid the fish tangling around them. The rod tip should be kept high so that the trout is pulling against the bend in the rod and not directly from the reel. I have seen anglers point the rod at the fish and crank the reel handle like crazy, not giving the fish a chance to make a run. By sheer good luck in many instances the trout is well hooked, winched right up to the rod tip, and an attempt made to lift it into the boat dangling on the end of the rod. A common remark in such cases is, 'Why don't you climb up the rod and stab him to death?' It is certainly no way to treat a plucky trout, nor, for that matter, a fine rod.

I called for a client one morning who was so looking forward to his fishing that he hadn't slept a wink all night. He was too full of excitement and anticipation—which, after all, is not a bad complaint, as I know several Casanovas who suffer the same way. He arrived down at the hotel foyer with six rods and thirteen reels, obviously prepared for any emergency. On board the boat he rigged up his favourite rod with a very expensive multiplying reel fitted with brakes and drags and paid out his line. I reached over and loosened the drag right off, so that if a trout should strike it would be able to take out the line. But he wasn't having any. He was anticipating monster trout and when he thought I wasn't looking he tightened the drag more and more, until eventually it must have been so tight a bulldozer wouldn't have budged it. The inevitable happened. A fish struck and pulled the rod clean out of his hands and over the side, where it hit the water with a dollar-rendering splash. Proof, I guess, of my advice about star drags. I dragged for and finally retrieved that rod and would like to say that when I pulled in the line the fish was still there. But it had long since departed, and gave my client the continuing story of the monster that got away.

Trolling reel holding lead line as fitted in rod-holder made by the author for his boat. Rod holders are illegal when there is more than one angler in the boat

The average trout will make two to three good long runs, each one shorter than the last. It will generally make a final run the moment it is brought close enough to see the boat, and a last valiant effort when it sees the net, so one should be ready for these, especially the last two. The crucial moment comes when the fish is brought close to the boat. I have seen hundreds of trout lost at this point. One must be extra careful not to wind in too much line or the line-to-leader knot will often catch in the tip guide and cause the trout and hook to part company. I always make sure that the entire cast and approximately 30 centimetres of line are still out through the rod tip guide. To bring the fish closer, hold the rod up high, even as far as pointing it back behind the shoulder. This method still gives the trout the bend in the rod for tension and prevents break-offs. A needle knot to join leader to line is highly recommended to prevent the above problems as I have had better success with it than normal knots.

NETTING THE TROUT

It is a mistake to approach the trout with the net from the tail end as the fish can swim away from it. It is best to net from the front as no trout can swim backwards.

52

The handle on the net should be a long one, preferably over a metre, so as to reach out for the fish.

It is also good policy to have the angler stand in the middle of the boat. This balances things better as all passengers are inclined to rush to the side where the fish is, giving the boat an awkward tilt.

TROLLING LIMITATIONS

Unlike fly fishing, where one can fish anywhere, trollers have a great many restrictions placed on them, so a good knowledge of the regulations is essential. In many areas it is illegal to use wire or lead lines; in others it is illegal to troll closer than 200 metres to the shoreline, or to a fisherman standing on shore; others still have a 300 metre restriction around stream mouths. It is illegal to travel faster than 8 km/h on any lake within 200 metres of the shore. It is also good policy to give water-ski lanes a wide berth, for not only may you get your line chopped off by a speeding propeller, but you could become very unpopular with water-skiers if they have to alter their run to avoid your slow-moving boat. A fly fisherman standing in water almost to the depth of his waders will also not take kindly to you if you go steaming past creating a wake that will swamp him.

When trolling in the vicinity of other boats who are also fishing, it is common courtesy to patrol back and forth paralleling the shoreline as they will be doing, and to make your turns away from and not into them, so as to prevent crossing lines. It is not good manners to take a line across the bows of another boat or to pursue an erratic course among them. A Marine Department law states that when two boats are approaching each other one should pass to the right of the other, not on the left as we do on the road. So it can be seen that when trolling there are a great many other things to consider, for as well as the law there is courtesy and respect for other lake users.

LURES FOR TROLLERS

Anyone walking into a sports store is likely to be completely floored by the array of different lures offered for sale. There is a theory that most of them are designed to catch the angler and not the fish, and judging by the number of useless and superfluous gadgets in my own tackle box I would say it is mostly true.

Over the years I have found fewer than a dozen that have proved themselves consistent fish catchers. The most popular are the Penny Spoon, Billy Hill, Mother of Pearl, Zed Spinner, Minnow, Toby, Cobra, Flatfish and Hot Shot. So a good tackle box should have at

The six most popular trolling and spinning lures used in New Zealand

(Left to right) Zed *Spinner, Flamingo, Black Toby, Tasmanian Devil, King Cobra, Cobra*

least one of each and preferably several of each in different colours and sizes. With metal spoons, red has been the most consistent fish-attracting colour, in either copper or brass.

I have never been able to work out why some lures have been tremendously successful for a couple of seasons and then almost overnight have been completely shunned by the trout. This has happened with many lures in my experience, and to fishing guides it is a popular topic of conversation. For instance, in the 1950s the Penny and Pearl were tremendously popular, but by the 1960s had been replaced by the Zed Spinner. For several years many anglers used nothing else until the Hot Shot and Flatfish appeared on the scene in the early 1970s. Today is the day of the Cobra, a lure with a wide range of colours and sizes which is now used almost exclusively by experienced trollers.

Despite lures coming and going, probably the most consistent over the entire period has been the Toby, always available in a wide range of colours and sizes. It rates as my favourite lure, with Cobra and Flatfish second, except for the Flatfish's notorious reputation (with its wide-course wobble action) for tangling lines. I prefer to use a Flatfish when I am on my own, or with two well spaced lines at the most.

Although these are the tried and proven fish catchers, there are new products appearing on the market all the time. One should never write off a funny-looking gadget merely from its looks; it could make you swallow your own smile, as I have often done. My favourite method of experimenting when I operated as a fishing guide was to give my two clients a rod and lure that had caught fish the day before. I would then run a third line myself and change the lure every ten to fifteen minutes, or until I achieved results. I would then hand it to a client, take his rod and repeat the process. Sometimes I would go through my entire collection of lures and then start on any new-fangled gadgets my clients had brought along. In this manner I often found an old lure that would gain a new lease of life, or a new lure from a client's tackle box that I would have bet my shirt wouldn't catch a trout.

Several trollers I know use nothing but flies and would never dream of towing 'hardware'. In fact, looking back through my diaries I find that flies were responsible for nearly fifty per cent of all my trolling catches. Lure or streamer flies are the most successful in sizes either six or four. The most popular are the Parsons' Glory, Taupo Tiger, Grey Ghost, Kilwell, Hamill's Killer and Mrs Simpson.

TACKLE FOR TROLLING

Tackle shops often recommend that trollers purchase short stiff boat rods—possibly a hangover from selling so many snapper rods to sea anglers. This, I feel, is a mistake. Short rods give no feel, have little bend, and the fish is almost pulling line directly from the reel. They are only one step better than using a hand line. My recommendation is for a long supple rod of not less than two metres in length. In fact, most of the top trolling guides only use fly rods for this purpose, which is proof of the pudding. A long rod will lose fewer fish, and long rods, fished in company, keep the lines further apart. All of my own trolling rods are made from old fly rods which have perhaps lost a few centimetres off the tip.

Reels for trolling should preferably be single-action. Normal fly reels are ideal, except that they will not hold enough line if using a full lead line. I dislike any form of star drag (another hangover from sea fishing) as these are more suited to short stiff rods. Any form of clutch or drag that allows line to be pulled from the reel while the handle is being turned is not necessary in trout fishing if a long rod is used. Nor is it very sporting. A client once remarked that he might as well use an electric winch.

Wire lines generally cause more trouble than they are worth, but trollers, being the great experimenters, will try them at least once, if only for the experience. The main trouble with them is that anglers attach them to a narrow-spool, large-diameter reel from which they are prone to lift off like a coiled spring during the overrun, often causing impossible tangles. The correct reel for wire lines is a wide-spool, bait-casting type, preferably fitted with a level-wind line-guide which runs back and forth and winds the line on to the reel spool in even layers. These of course are much more expensive but are well worth the added cost, if only for peace of mind—if you really must fish with a wire line. As well, glass insert rings in the line-guides on the rod are essential, as the wire will wear deep grooves and eventually work right through normal metal rings.

The majority of trollers use a leader of the same length they employ in fly fishing, i.e. the length of the rod. This was o.k. in the days of few boats, but today, with a new breed of line-shy trout, a longer leader has been found much more efficient. For over ten years now the top trolling guides have been using leaders measuring at least 9 metres. A swivel should not be used with flies but is most essential with any spinning lure to prevent line twist.

For boating a trout, the landing net is most favoured, for although gaffs are still used they are illegal in many districts. A round, deep-meshed net is preferable, and it should have a handle not less than 1.2 metres (4 ft) long.

For storing the fish aboard the boat there are now some very good plastic fish bins available. These are much preferred over tossing the trout into the outboard well or bilge, where it will get caught up in the steering cables or flop around in oil. I cover the fish with a wet sack or towel, which keeps them fresh and clean at the same time.

To round off the tackle requirements, every boat should have a fish-killer for dispatching the trout quickly and humanely. I have seen these made from police truncheons, the handle of a billiard cue, a Maori mere, or the good old standby, a crescent spanner. To kill a trout quickly, there is a slight depression just behind the head where the hard bone-like structure of the head gives way to the softer flesh of the back. Place the trout belly down in the fish bin and give it a couple of sharp whacks on this spot.

I was fishing once on Lake Wakatipu with Jim Conway, making a movie for his television outdoor show in Portland, Oregon. The fishing was tough, and after exhausting all my efforts of literally 'throwing the book at them', Jim started on a few favourite tricks of his own—we badly needed a big brown. He pulled forth from the depths of his tackle box what is known in the United States as a 'Ford Fender', a short length (60 cm or 2 ft) of piano wire with a swivel at each end. Spaced about every 10 centimetres along it are swivels with little spoons attached and these spin around the wire like tiny propellers; between the spinners are alternate brightly-coloured beads. It is a teaser and is tied on the line about a metre ahead of the lure, the object being that the trout is first attracted by it, then gets excited about the whole thing, and finally spots the lure, which by this time looks irresistible.

My Kiwi colleague and I looked on with highly amused expressions as Jim assembled this monstrosity, as neither of us at that time had ever seen one before. To cap it all off, he attached a 10-cm yellow flatfish with brown spots—we had never seen one of these before either. Both of us in our wisdom assured Jim that he would never catch anything except a cold with such a contraption. Nevertheless, over the side went the whole caboodle, and the whole process was accompanied by much jocularity.

He had scarcely paid out 50 metres of line, when whamm!—unbelievable, he had a fish on. You never saw two smiles disappear so quickly. The water of Lake Wakatipu is beautifully clear and as Jim brought the fish closer to the boat we could see down about 5 metres where the brown was fighting the hook and flashing its sides at us. What was more remarkable still was to see another brown trout rush in from the sidelines and begin attacking the teaser. Incredible! I was sold on the idea then and there. With an outfit like that, I thought, I'd be able to catch fish in the bath. I promptly ordered several teasers from the United States in assorted sizes and colours, but the sad fact is that I have never caught a trout using one. One quickly loses patience with them; they are clumsy to use, weigh a ton in the water and give you a sore arm holding the rod against the drag on the line. The moral, though, is that one never stops learning in this trolling caper.

Stan Potts, the veteran Rotorua guide, was trolling with a client one day when the fishing was tough. The conversation lagged; it looked

like a long hungry winter. The client after a lengthy silence announced that the only way to catch a fish in those conditions was to buy one. 'Never fails,' he added, as he tossed a fifty-cent piece over the side. The coin hit the rod tip, which twanged musically, and zap! a trout struck at that moment and zipped out the line.

'We landed that fish,' said Stan, 'and then the client proceeded to toss all the change in his pocket over the side, plus all of mine, along with a few choice words. We never caught another fish all day.'

Stan's explanation is that the twang as the coin hit the rod tip changed the speed of the lure and caused the fish to strike, as it could have been following the lure for quite a while. A spurt in the lure speed could cause the trout to think it was getting away, another good reason for changing trolling speed occasionally.

If that's not incredible enough, Stan was trolling on Lake Rotorua one morning with an Australian client and using fly lines. The outboard motor died on them and they immediately wound in their lines and stowed them, but the client left his fly and line dangling in the lake. Stan was busy changing plugs when all of a sudden a rainbow weighing 1.5 kg jumped clean into the boat and started thrashing around amid the tackle. You can imagine their surprise when they finally grasped the fish to find that it was hooked legally; the fly on the client's line was embedded firmly in its mouth.

My most memorable trolling trip started off from the old Grand Hotel, Rotorua, where I arrived to pick up a lady angler one morning at half past four. I had mentioned on the phone that we would be back for breakfast by 8.30. She turned up in the hotel foyer dressed in flared cocktail skirt, silk stockings, high-heeled shoes complete with wide-brimmed picture hat—the works. You never know your luck in the guiding game.

We headed out on to the lake and had time to catch only one fish before the rain started and the wind blew up rough and us off the lake. Arriving back at the hotel at half past six, long before we were expected, she insisted that I accompany her to their room and bring the fish to show her husband. On entering the room, it turned out that hubby had been doing a little fishing of his own with a younger female member of their party. My client, looking around for something to throw at them, seized on the trout, then proceeded to chase the lovers round the room, sloshing at them with the fish at every chance she got, accompanying her actions with a few choice words completely new to me and a shower of fish scales. It was certainly no way to treat a noble trout, but it was worth the price of admission for a front-row view of the action. . . . Such are the thrills of trolling.

(Opposite) *Author's daughter Lorraine with four fine rainbows taken in Stump Bay, Lake Taupo, on a morning's trolling trip*

Spinning
and
Baitcasting

Spinning and baitcasting reels are designed to cast a heavy lure or spinner and are extremely popular in the U.S.A., where they are ideally suited to bass fishing. Baitcasting reels were very popular in New Zealand before World War II, but after that, spinning or fixed-spool reels gained in popularity and have now more or less replaced them. Because both types of reel were little known when most of our fishing regulations were devised, many of the best fishing locations are designated 'fly only', which means that there is limited use for both types in many areas. However, it is a popular style of fishing, particularly in rivers that flow to the sea in both islands of New Zealand. Before using this tackle, I recommend checking the regulations to make sure it is legal in the district concerned.

BAITCASTING REELS

Baitcasting reels were designed in the U.S.A. before the turn of the century for casting 'live' bait, hence the name 'Baitcaster'. They are a revolving-spool reel which runs free during the cast but engages a clutch the moment the handle is turned for the retrieve. Some dexterity and skill are required, as the thumb is used to apply pressure to the spool during the cast to avoid backlash and overwind. Like the spinning reel, they have a slipping clutch mechanism which allows the handle to be cranked while the fish is still peeling off line. One advantage over spinning reels is that it does not twist the line at each turn of the handle, and for this reason I consider it the better reel. Once the technique of thumb control has been mastered, it is a very easy and trouble-free reel to use.

SPINNING REELS

The first patent on a spinning reel was taken out in England before 1900 by a man named Illingworth, but since then the reel has been improved by manufacturers throughout the world. It is a fixed-spool reel placed at right angles to the rod so that the line peels off the spool in coils. The first line-guide on a spin rod has a large ring to allow these coils to flow freely through it.

There are two types of spinning reel. One is a closed-face reel which sits on top of the rod and, like a baitcaster, has a thumb button to control backlash and overwind. The other type, the open-face reel, hangs below the rod and is often referred to as a threadline reel. It does not have any form of thumb control. The latter is by far the most popular in New Zealand, mainly because it will hold more line than the closed-face reel and tangles are easier to sort out. It is also easier to operate. Both types have a drag and slipping clutch which allows the handle to be cranked while the fish is peeling off line, but when the fish slows his run the continual winding will gather line.

Some anglers often call this 'automatic' fishing and dislike the system after having been brought up in the single-action fly-reel tradition. In actual fact, when a fish is taking out line and the handle is turned, a twist will form in the line and if this is continued the monofilament will become a mass of twists and tangles, making casting impossible. Few professional guides will use this reel with

A river 'just made for shooting-head lines and streamer flies'—the Tongariro at a popular spot known as the Red Hut pool

Spinning reels. Top: *Closed-face spinning reel—note how handle is angled with trigger grip, which allows thumb to work overrun button.* Middle: *Open-face spinning reel Mitchell model 301 reel with bale.* Bottom: *Baitcasting reel with handle also angled so that the thumb can be applied to the line on the reel spool to prevent overwind*

inexperienced clients for that reason. It is much better to apply fly-fishing principles when using this reel and only crank the handle when the fish is giving way, letting it go when the fish is peeling off line. Twists will then disappear. However, the design of the reel does not encourage this type of self control.

THE RETRIEVE

The retrieve with spinning and baitcasting tackle is not controlled in the free hand as in fly fishing, but is done by rewinding the line on to the reel. This allows for variations of speed, ensuring that the lure will work through the water with action. Before I start fishing with it, I always toss any lure out a short distance so that I can watch it moving through the water and adjust my retrieve to get it working at the right speed. This is most important, because some lures require a fast retrieve and others a very slow one.

FISHING WITH SPINNING AND BAITCASTING TACKLE

Fishing with this tackle allows for extreme accuracy in tossing lures
and spinners into lakes and rivers and into places which are often
impossible to reach with a fly rod. It makes a useful addition to any
angler's tackle collection. It is not suitable for fly fishing, although I
have noticed an increasing number of anglers using a plastic bubble
on the line ahead of the fly. The bubble is filled with water, giving it
the necessary weight to toss a fly a long distance. In many districts
this tube is classified as a weight and it is illegal in 'fly only' areas.
Regulations should be checked before such a device is used.

A spinning outfit is ideal for taking on outback camping trips into
remote areas as a means of producing a tasty trout, as there are many
pools in the mountains that have never seen an angler. Using this
tackle, one does away with the decision-making about what type of
fly to use or the feeding habits of the fish. Almost any spinner or lure
in remote areas should entice an unwary trout.

Popular lures are the Minnow, Zed Spinner, Toby, Billy Hill and
Mother of Pearl. Other lighter lures such as the Cobra and Flatfish can
be used, but usually need a weight attached to obtain distance.

Of recent years spin tackle outfits have become a favourite present
from parents to youngsters as their first rod. This has one advantage
in that they are simple to use and will catch fish easily, giving the
youngster encouragement to graduate to other methods. However, I
would rather see it the other way round and the youngster receive a
fly rod as his first outfit. He can graduate to spinning in later years
and will be a far better fisherman for it.

To show the effectiveness of spinning in a strange area, an
American walked into my office one afternoon recently and asked
where he could catch a trout with a spinning outfit. I advised him to
drive out and fish the Waikato River at Mihi between Rotorua and
Taupo. That same afternoon, as I called at a dairy for a newspaper, I
bumped into the same bloke staggering out of the shop with an
armful of bacon, mushrooms, onions, bread and eggs, and a large
satisfied grin on his face. 'Come and have a look in my car,' he said,
and there lying in the boot was a fat brown trout weighing 2 kg. He
had taken it on his second cast just upstream of the Mihi bridge. He
and his wife immediately booked into a motel so that they could cook
the fish.

In the late 1960s I was given the job of finding suitable scenic
locations for a comedy trout-fishing movie using well known local
actors. One scene called for a sports car to scream up to the edge of a
lake in a cloud of dust, whereupon a young inexperienced angler was

to jump out and assemble a brand-new rod while still wearing his city clothes. He was in a race to catch a rainbow trout. The funny scene was to follow as he made his first cast. The spoon was to get stuck in a tree and as it came loose he was to clout himself on the back of the head with it.

I found the perfect spot on the edge of Lake Taupo, and when the day arrived, camera crews and actors gathered at the scene for a dummy run. Everything went according to plan and the next time was to be the dinkum oil. Out came the clapper board, 'Scene 17, Take 1', and the action was on. The car screamed to a halt, the actor jumped out, assembled the rod and began to cast furiously. The spoon caught in the tree, he hit himself on the back of the head and everyone was beginning to laugh. It was funny. The star then walked into the lake where he was supposed to fish . . . and disappeared completely out of sight. Only his hat was left floating on the water. He came up blowing like a surfacing whale to find all the camera crew rolling on the ground in hysterics. The scene was so funny it was added to the script. The only thing I had neglected in my scene-finding, was to test the depth of the water, but that was one time when a mistake turned into a gold strike.

A few short years ago I received a cable from the *Mariposa* cruise liner, a day out of Auckland, to arrange two one-day fish and hunt excursions. Two sportsmen had a competition going, with a bet on the side, that they would leave the ship when it docked in the morning and return the same evening, one with a deer and the other with a trout. They were so sure of New Zealand's sporting reputation that they had even ordered a banquet for the following night, alerted the chef and invited the captain. I cabled a reply that I could arrange the deal and set about organising suitable guides. I booked a hunting guide to pick the hunter up from shipside and take him to the King Country for the day. I then arranged for the fisherman to be flown by amphibian from Mechanics Bay to Lake Okataina, where a guide would meet him by boat to take him fishing on the lake. That evening I phoned the hunting guide to check on the success or failure of the mission. They had fired at a deer but missed. Rather apprehensively I then phoned Allan Beamish-White at Lake Okataina to see how the angler had made out. 'Oh, the deerfishin' was fine,' Allan said. They had gone out spinning and caught three fine rainbows up to 3 kg and on the way home had roped a deer which was swimming across the lake. I would hazard a guess that there is one very happy deer/angler who is still dining out on that story.

(Opposite) *ex-president Jimmy Carter of the USA hugs Margarette Coutts, proprietor of Tongariro Fishing Lodge (who also happens to be a top fly fisherwoman) in his delight at catching this fine 3.62 kg (8 lb) rainbow hen from the Tongariro delta*

Myth and Fact about Fishing in New Zealand

New Zealand has often been described as the 'great fish factory', for from Lake Taupo alone 500 tonnes of trout are taken annually by 70,000 licensed anglers. In a recent year, during a local competition at Taupo, 271 trout were weighed in for a total of 533 kg, an average weight close on 2 kg per fish. Similarly, at Rotorua during a week-long competition, 1389 trout were weighed in totalling 2075 kg, an average of 1.5 kg. Throughout both contests trout of 3 to 4.5 kg were caught every day. So the claim that there are more 'four-pound trout' (2 kg) caught in New Zealand on an angler-to-fish basis than anywhere else in the world is probably correct.

With the growth of both guiding and tourism, more and more anglers are coming to New Zealand to try their luck. Guides estimate that 5000 visiting anglers are taking about 15,000 trout annually, and considering that the majority of visitors fish for only a couple of hours each, the success ratio is pretty high. A myth has therefore grown in overseas countries that New Zealand is overwhelmed with trout—that you have almost to hide behind a tree in order to bait the hooks. Anyone travelling here with that idea in mind is obviously going to be disappointed.

New Zealand is a small country with a sparse population and a sparser-still angling population, but with a large amount of available trout water. The trout are officially managed on a fish to food-supply to angling-pressure basis, almost the same as a farm is managed. This way we should not have too many fish that are too small, nor too few that are too large. A balance is achieved as far as possible by increasing or decreasing seasons, thus allowing angling pressure to kill off overpopulations and vice versa.

The system is working quite well, especially in lakes like Tarawera, Rotorua and Taupo, where the average weights have remained almost constant for a number of years. These average weights for trout are 0.9–1.4 kg (2–3 lb) in Lake Rotorua, 1.4–1.8 kg (3–4 lb) in Lake Taupo and 0.9–1.8 kg (2–4 lb) in most of the South Island. In Lake Tarawera trout weighing 3.6–4.5 kg (8–10 lb) are caught annually, and this is also true of Lake Taupo and most of the South Island. Occasionally really big fish are taken, such as the 10.4 kg (23 lb) brown caught by a schoolboy in the lower Waikato River, or the 9 kg (20 lb) brown caught by Tom Gilmour at Lake Waituna. Every year sees numbers of trout weighing 5–10 kg caught in both islands.

So in this country we have the happy situation of having many areas where the trout are reasonably big as distinct from areas absolutely teeming with small trout. This means, however, that there is a lot of water between each fish and that the angler will not catch large numbers of fish here unless he strikes conditions absolutely

(Opposite) Two Californian anglers with 'wilderness monsters' from the famed Rangitikei River caught in 1978. Kerney Towers (left) with a 3.3-kg rainbow and Charlie Carniglia with a 3.6-kg rainbow. These large trout are average for this river (see page 144)

70

right. A fly fisherman will consider it a good day if he catches one or two good browns on a dry in a South Island stream, or four good rainbows on a wet fly in a North Island lake. Trollers usually fare better, but limit bags of eight trout a day are something to talk about. The tourist angler, therefore, must realise that he cannot expect quantity in New Zealand, but he will certainly get quality.

It is a well known fact that visiting anglers fishing with guides have in recent times been obtaining better fishing than most local anglers. We receive what we pay for and a top guide will undoubtedly make the difference between a good and bad tour. Yet it still amazes me how many anglers travel so far and spend so much money getting here only to economise at this end and try to go it alone.

Another myth pertaining throughout the angling world is that fishing is easy in this country. I have never found it so. If it comes to that, good fishing has a way of deserving a good fisherman and one who is not a successful angler at home will fare little better in another country. A visiting angler wishing to fish with streamer fly, should be able to cast a line 20 metres (70 ft) plus. It is a fact that without this ability the results will be pretty poor.

There is also an old proverb, 'When in Rome, do as the Romans do.' This is never more true than in fishing. Guides could write books on the number of clients who have ignored local advice and pulled out lures that have 'slaughtered 'em' back home but caught no fish here. I have a drawer full of such lures that haven't turned the fish on at all. The best way to try out new lures is when the fishing is good and you have already caught several on proved methods. Then by all means try out the new ones—you have nothing to lose and a lot to gain.

Visiting anglers fall into two categories, mainly those who fish occasionally while here on a sightseeing tour and those who come especially to fish. The first kind generally hire guides during a stop-off at a lake resort and are taken trolling. These visitors usually have 100 per cent success. They catch by far the most fish, mainly because they are not fussy about how they fish and are accompanied by guides who were fishing yesterday.

On the other hand, the angler coming especially to fly-fish may have problems. If, for instance, he is on his first visit, he will probably want to fish and see both islands, North and South. His reading about New Zealand will have told him that there is excellent dry-fly fishing for browns on the Mataura and excellent wet-fly fishing for rainbows on the Tongariro. He would like to fish both. The difficulty here is that when the Tongariro is fishing well, the majority of the South Island is closed to fishing. Again, if he arrives during the

Ted Trueblood, famous U.S. angling writer, with a 3.2 kg (7 lb) rainbow taken near the influx of the Waihaha Stream, Western Bay, Taupo

popular visitor vacation months, November to December and February to March, the dry-fly fishing will be excellent in the South Island but the wet-fly rainbow fishing in the popular requested areas of the North Island will all be in lakes. I find that purist fly anglers from overseas do not like lake fishing, even though it is good and they are in 'Rome'. So fishing both islands in the popular areas can only be a compromise.

My suggestion is to advise your travel agent exactly what sort of fishing is your main interest, and also to state your second alternative. It helps, too, if you can let him know just how good you are at your chosen sport, all modesty aside. I receive requests about fishing every day, and if I have the above three main facts I can do my best to advise the angler when to come, where to go and who to go with, so as to make sure he is in the right place at the right time, with due allowance made for alternatives.

I am always being told that the fishing has deteriorated or is no longer as good as it used to be, mainly by 'pot' anglers who do nothing for future generations and take more than they need. Stories like that are for the past; they prove nothing. It's the future we as anglers in this country are concerned about. Granted that angling pressure is catching up with fish supply, yet there are many areas where the fishing is as good, if not better, than it ever was. There are still some areas that have seldom seen an angler, and in general we are going to have really good fishing for generations to come. If you want proof of this, all you have to do is drop in on taxidermists throughout this country. They have deepfreezes literally bulging with trout waiting to be mounted. Only last season I visited several that were full of rainbows and browns from 2 to 9 kg (4–20 lb), with the majority in the 2.7 to 6.8 kg class (6–15 lb). The quality is certainly here.

We who fish regularly find that we have excellent fishing almost on our doorsteps. We can catch more trout than we really need, and we are not yet overcrowded with fishermen—unless one likes fishing in a crowd. I believe we have the best trout fishing in the world, and it is my sincere hope that this book will help you enjoy this resource to the full.

I once took an English lord fishing. Strangely enough, he had never handled a rod in his life before, not even as a child, so I took him trolling. After a successful day of it, he sat back in the boat, a bottle in one hand and a rod in the other, with a contented smile on his face and remarked, 'This fishing, don't you know, is rather like wine. Once you've had a taste of it, you can't leave it alone.' I guess that sums up New Zealand fishing for me too.

(Opposite) *Ernie Schweibert, another prominent U.S. angling writer, plays a big rainbow in the Greenstone River, west of Lake Wakatipu*

Fishing
Guides
in
New Zealand

Just about everyone who has ever fished was taken out on his first few excursions by his father or grandfather, or just by a friend. In later years it is often easy to forget that you yourself first needed a guide, but the fact that you are still fishing proves that someone helped to make sure those first lessons were well learnt. New Zealand has had guides as long as there has been sport fishing; they have been used by locals and visitors alike because they save both time and money and add considerably to the success of a vacation.

I drifted into guiding mainly by chance. At the time it seemed the only logical thing to do and I have never regretted one exciting moment of it. My life has been pretty colourful one way or another, and for all of it I have been tied up in some way with either fishing or hunting. From 1945 to 1954 I was first a self-employed deerskin hunter, a Government deerculler, then a field officer hiring and supervising deercullers. I then moved to ranging work, catching wildlife lawbreakers as well as doing my share of work in hatcheries and on game farms. By 1954 I was again self-employed, catching opossums for bounty and selling venison to hotels. Things were going well for me; opossums had paid off my mortgage, put money in the bank and I had my first Landrover.

About this time I began receiving inquiries from hotels and local sports stores asking me if I could take their clients out hunting and fishing. Tourism was then in its post-war infancy, and as the demands grew I considered making it a full-time effort. These increasing demands, coupled with the fact that the Government was threatening to discontinue the opossum bounty scheme, finally persuaded me, and I launched the first 'All New Zealand Safaris'. Here at least was something that allowed me to do the things I liked doing and knew how to; getting rich was then very much a secondary consideration. I ran a fishing boat for charters on Lake Rotorua for four seasons, and in addition conducted hunting and fishing safaris throughout both islands of New Zealand. Strangely enough, hunting clients at the start far outnumbered fishing clients. Today this situation is reversed—angling clients now far outnumber the hunters, which shows the ever-increasing popularity of trout fishing.

By 1965 I had guided thousands of tourists from all over the world and had gained a good deal of the knowledge and first-hand experiences which I put into my first book, *Hunter for Hire* (Reed). This sold well and encouraged me to write my second book, *Hunting in New Zealand* (Reed), which is still available in its fifth edition. Altogether I had spent almost ten years adventuring and nearly

John Case, outdoors commentator for CBS Radio of Chicago, shows the results of jigging with a spin rod from Simon Dickie's anchored launch in Western Bay, Lake Taupo

another ten guiding around the country, and my business had grown to such an extent that I was never home. Some of my safaris kept me on the road and in the bush for as long as six weeks. This was tough on my family, so almost overnight I quit—like all my momentous decisions, it was sudden. I had been too busy to take my four children hunting, fishing or camping, so started enjoying a bushman's holiday. I owed them something and the personal satisfaction was tremendous. My vacation was short-lived, however, for within six months I was back into the hunting and fishing business facing greater demands than ever.

In 1965 the Tourist and Publicity Department had taken a long look at the guiding situation in New Zealand and decided that there were no standards, no licensing and no coordination. The whole thing was in a sad state, with few or no guides in areas where tourists would require them. In fact, at that time there was only one fishing guide in Rotorua, none at Turangi/Tokaanu, only six at Taupo and two in the entire length of the South Island. The hunting guide situation was equally sad. New Zealand was rapidly gaining a reputation as a place to hunt and fish, and it was obvious that the available guides could not cope with the numbers of interested tourist sportsmen. Something had to be done, and quickly.

I was offered and accepted the job of hunting and fishing officer and given the task of coordinating the country's guiding services and resources. The information I gained was then to be passed on to agents engaged in promoting and selling this sporting attraction. This meant listing all guides, encouraging new ones to set up in business in new areas, assisting them with promotion, and finally inspecting them all to make sure they could provide what they advertised. It was an interesting challenge and one in which my past experience was to prove very useful.

From that beginning the guiding industry has grown and kept pace with the tremendous annual increase in tourism. As one guide

Slim Whitman, U.S. country and western singer, and Rea Potts, internationally known trout-fishing guide, with a morning's bag taken from Lake Rotorua

80

became established and attracted business there would be room for another, and so on. This was the pattern that emerged until the guiding force found its own level of supply and demand. Over the next few years I assisted more than sixty guides to become established in popular areas, places either made famous by guides or where visiting anglers wished to go.

Looking back now, the greatest part of my time was spent answering correspondence from inquiring anglers and eventually designing tours for them or their travel agents. The Tourist and Publicity Department was keen to ensure that if a sports angler was willing to travel many thousands of miles to enjoy our fishing, he should be advised to go to the right place at the right time and fish

Bruce Steward, expert fly-fishing guide, holds up a fine Tongariro rainbow. Looking on is Tony Jensen, recently retired after many years successful guiding

81

with the right guide. This was not as difficult as it may sound, for our guide force is made up of individualists with different angling methods and types of equipment suited to different districts and types of water. No matter what kind of request—and some of them were mind-boggling—there was always a guide somewhere in New Zealand with both the ability and know-how to handle the job.

I have now sold thousands of tours to anglers from all over the world and the revenue 'intake' has certainly given the national economy a nudge in the right direction. The greatest benefit, however, has been to New Zealand's reputation as an anglers' paradise, though this has owed far more to the ingenuity, personality and good old 'Kiwi know-how' of the guides themselves. By world standards the ability of New Zealand fishing guides is second to none.

My job has naturally kept me away from active guiding, but on the other hand I have been given jobs like escorting overseas fishing writers, editors and television teams. All of these have been promotional efforts and as well as accompanying most of the editors of well known outdoor magazines, who have since published excellent articles on the fishing in this country, I have assisted in the making of about twenty half-hour television programmes, some of which are still showing overseas. During this period I also made five tours to the U.S.A., lecturing one-night stands to angling and outdoor clubs across the country to promote New Zealand's sporting attractions. All of which has given me a tremendous amount of personal satisfaction and many memorable and, on occasion, hilarious experiences.

SOME GUIDING EXPERIENCES

Ever been fishing with $100,000 worth of bulldozer? I'll tell you how it was accomplished. It was in my early years of guiding and a good fishing friend, Jack Stafford, was then bulldozing the road system and making the now famous marina at Kinloch in Western Bay, Lake Taupo. He phoned me one night to say that every time he pushed a cut from the swamp out to the lake, the trout would almost climb up the beach to get at the millions of tadpoles.

'Just let me know if you have a client who wants some out-of-this-world fishing and I'll breach the swamp the night before,' he said. As it happened, I had a client who had asked me to guide him one day on the Rotorua lakes and one day at Taupo, so I asked Jack to let the cut out the next evening. Just as well I did, for the fishing on Lake Rotorua next day was a fizzer and by late afternoon we were almost at the stage of seeking permission to fish in Fairy Springs. That evening Jack cranked up his bulldozer and drained the swamp into the lake; he even came round later and gave me some flies he had made to resemble tadpoles—I later named them 'Jackpole' flies.

The next morning my client, an American admiral, and I arrived at the end of the Kinloch pumice road just at dawn, and when I took a look at the rip caused by the outlet of the swamp flowing into the lake, I couldn't believe my eyes. The trout were packed in the current with their dorsal and tail fins sticking out of the water. It is only on rare occasions one sees sights like this and Jack's tadpole and bulldozer trick was obviously working. I tied a 'Jackpole' on each of our lines and instructed my client not to walk into the water but fish from the beach, adding that if he struck a fish, he should walk down the beach and lead the trout away so that it would not disturb the others.

His first cast hooked him into a leaping rainbow and mine did likewise. This set the pattern for an action-packed morning. In one hour my client's arm was aching from holding a bent rod; in two hours he was looking not only dazed and exhausted but bewildered—he couldn't believe it. We never counted the total but by mid-morning we estimated we had taken some fifty rainbows averaging about two kilograms (4 lb). We returned all to the water and only kept three for the pan. We'd had enough and packed our rods, but couldn't tear ourselves away, for as we sat on the beach demolishing a can or two of 'turps' trout were still surfacing in the rip. The admiral confessed he had come a long way to find good fishing but never in his wildest dreams did he think it would be like this. I did not tell him about the bulldozer or Jack; he thought the fishing was like that all the time. Unfortunately guides don't always have it so good.

One of the greatest stunts I ever had a hand in was arranging a trout-fishing trip for one I like to call the 'fish and chip girl'. In England an expatriate New Zealander was working on a television programme run along quiz-show lines, and he never missed an opportunity to put in a free plug where he could for 'Godzone'. On this occasion a young nurse won a parcel of fish and chips and on opening the parcel found some chips and a return air ticket to New Zealand to catch the trout to go with them. The idea was great and it snowballed. It was decided to send a film crew with her so that her exploits catching the fish could be shown the following Saturday night on the same programme. This was widened to include as much scenery in New Zealand as possible to take advantage of the free advertising—Milford Sound, a ski-plane landing at Mount Cook and the geysers and trout springs at Rotorua. All in all a tremendous

Simon Dickie, world-famous fishing guide from Lake Taupo, poses with a 4.76 kg (10.5 lb) rainbow taken in the Rangitikei River during an early exploratory trip to this famous and remote river

publicity promotion, except it didn't allow much time for catching the trout, the prime reason for her journey.

I was contacted to arrange the fishing at Rotorua and nearly swallowed a fly when I found how little time was allocated. She was to arrive on the noon flight and depart on the 2.30 p.m. one, and in that short time was to catch a trout, have it cooked in a hangi, and visit the geysers and the trout springs. Everyone knows that the noon hours are the worst for fishing, and on top of that she had probably never fished before and was pretty certain to lose a fish even if she

84

hooked one. Well, fishing guides do the impossible right now; miracles take a little longer. . . . After a few sleepless nights, I came to the conclusion that some form of 'insurance' would definitely be required.

On the morning of the attempt I managed to get two live trout and kept them swimming in a pen in the lake. As the hour drew near, these were transferred to a can full of water, with an oxygen bottle feeding life-giving air into the water. Stan Potts was enlisted as guide and he smuggled the can aboard his launch only seconds before the entourage arrived from the airport. Meanwhile hundreds of spectators had turned up on hearing of the event over the local radio, plus umpteen reporters, photographers and radio announcers, who proceeded to hire every available speed boat and launch at the wharf. I had already dispatched another trout from my deepfreeze to Whakarewarewa, where it went into the hangi around 12.30 p.m. so as to be cooked when the girl and camera crew arrived.

A flotilla of boats headed out into the lake, for all the world like a regatta on the Waitemata Harbour. Despite speed boats whizzing around us like bees about a hive, all merrily snapping photos, we did make a genuine attempt to catch a trout. Several lines were paid out but within minutes they were chopped off by the propellers of eager reporters. Stan and I, realising that the odds were heavily stacked against us, gave each other the silent nod and began the great switcheroo.

We were taking a gamble which daren't go wrong, and no one, especially the nurse, must know what was taking place. Stan, acting like the old pro he is, quietly whipped a live trout from the can, hooked it on to a fly and bent the hook so that it couldn't possibly come out. I meanwhile attracted everyone's attention at the stern of the boat. When there were no boats passing on the blind side, Stan dropped the trout out of the side window, paid out fifty metres of line, and passed the rod round the side of the boat to me. I suggested to the young lady that she try another rod for luck and switched rods on her. She only held the new one for a moment before the trout leapt clean out of the water—right on cue, it couldn't have performed better.

Miraculously no one witnessed Stan and I at our little game, though there were a few mystified expressions among the locals. The trout was duly brought to the boat ('winched' would be a better word) and netted, then photographed to death with victory smiles all round. The little nurse was overwhelmed. She couldn't believe her luck and the look on her face was a treat to see.

On returning to the wharf, we threaded our way through the

throng of spectators, boarded the line-up of cars and headed for Whaka. After filming the girl viewing geysers and boiling mud pools, we arrived at the hangi site where the trout was brought forth cooked to perfection and promptly devoured by a hungry group.

'Is this really my own trout?' she asked.

'Of course,' was the reply. 'You have to get up early to beat a Kiwi.'

At least Stan and I, like politicians, agreed that we had acted in the best interests of our country.

GUIDES IN NEW ZEALAND TODAY

In the early days of guiding in this country the term for a sportsman's attendant was a 'gillie', an imported Scottish word that did not fit well with the Kiwi character, being far too servile. In Britain fishing water can cost thousands of dollars and the gillie is thrown in along with the receipt, rather like a servant. Here the fly is stuck in the other ear; the water is free but the guide comes expensive, as he runs a business and has no lord or master except the tax department.

A good example of this was forthcoming when a British admiral was visiting Wellington and requested a day's fishing on Lake Taupo. Ron Houghton's launch was chartered for the admiral's party, which consisted of sundry captains and lieutenants. Ron ran a smart ship, everything in top working order, and cooked the best meals on the lake, as well as being an expert and knowledgeable fisherman. The fishing turned out excellent and as noon approached the admiral dispatched a lieutenant to inform Ron that lunch should be prepared. He dropped anchor in a calm bay and, while the official party quaffed gins on deck, prepared his usual excellent lunch. Then the lieutenant was back to inform Ron that the admiral's party would dine alone, and would he vacate the cabin.

'You go back and tell the admiral that on my ship the captain sits at his own table,' Ron informed him, whereupon the party filed in and sat down to an appetising lunch. The admiral learnt that in New Zealand trout fishing is the great equaliser.

Guiding is usually a one-man operation, providing car, outboard boat or launch and all necessary tackle. The boat will require a Ministry of Transport (Marine Division) survey and the guide will need a launchmaster's ticket to drive it. His car will have a passenger service licence and the client is fully covered by insurance. On an average the guide will be placing at his client's disposal anything from $30,000 to $150,000 worth of equipment, along with his greatest asset, his experience and know-how, for as little as $40 to $70 per hour, a pretty reasonable deal.

Alister Benfield, guide and proprietor of Lake Rotoroa Lodge in Nelson, releases a 1.36 kg (3 lb) brown trout in the Gowan River adjacent to the popular lodge

Gary Kemsley, popular Taupo fly-fishing guide and outdoors writer poses with a 4.76 kg (10.5 lb) hen rainbow trout taken from Lake Otomangakau in 1983

There are two types of guides, those who go into the business for the money and those who go into it for the love of the game, with monetary gain a secondary consideration. The former mostly become disillusioned, as I have yet to meet a rich guide; the latter, by far, make the best guides. I have seen many hopefuls come and go in the last twenty years, mainly because guiding is not lucrative and because of the very short, six-month season, bearing in mind that the busy tourist season only accounts for about four of those months. Skill at fishing his own area is most essential, but is not enough if he doesn't have the personality and popularity to go along with it. A guide has a four-year trial period. If he is any good at his vocation, by the end of that time he will generally be attracting enough business to give him a reasonable living. If, on the other hand, he is not making a living, he generally gets the message and tries his hand at something else. It's a highly competitive business.

The guide provides a pick-up and drop-off service from hotel or airport to the fishing venue and endeavours to take the client to the best local area at the right time. He never fishes himself unless the client asks him to. After all, the client is doing the paying and should be the one to catch the fish. A guide is expected to be travel agent, barman, message boy, philosopher, teacher and father confessor, as well as a bloke to blame, lean on or get drunk with. He gets paid for eight hours, often works twelve, and many times blows his day's profit in a bar with tomorrow's client. If you don't weaken, it's a great life.

Guides have done a lot of good for New Zealand. They have taught many people to fish and many anglers owe their introduction to fishing to a guide. In their turn they have learnt from their clients and many of the methods used in this country today were passed on to guides, who duly passed them on to local anglers. One of their greatest achievements has been conservation, and in this regard methods adopted by guides are now being used by anglers everywhere. New Zealanders have been brought up in a land of plenty and a common occurrence at one time was to see anglers catching limit bags and staggering home with sackfuls of fish, not really sure what to do with them. A new guide's first shock, having been brought up in this tradition, is to watch an American client throwing back live fish, for the American will have been raised in circumstances where anglers are taught to conserve. After the initial surprise, most guides take kindly to this idea and start practising it themselves. It is common now to see guides all over New Zealand returning live unwanted trout to the water and, more encouraging still, to know that as a result other local anglers are doing the same. There is no doubt that the dollar earnings from tourist anglers have assisted this country, but to my mind the conservation techniques brought by these visiting anglers have been just as beneficial.

My recommendation to people undecided about hiring a guide is to take the plunge every time. Since he has survived that four-year trial period, he will be a pretty good bloke to know. The chances are that he will have been fishing yesterday, so will know where to take you today. He'll take most of the gamble out of fishing for you, and on top of that give you an interesting and enjoyable day with lasting memories of a successful vacation.

Suggested Equipment for Visiting Anglers

Hire tackle is not available at all fishing locations. In particular the hiring out of waders has proved to be unprofitable. Anglers in hired waders burst through blackberry bushes with gay abandon and leave leaks for the next hirer to find, making them unreliable.

If you contemplate hiring guides for all your fishing, there will be no need to bring any tackle as they can provide everything you want. But if you intend hiring guides for only part of the time or wish to fish entirely on your own, it will be advisable to have your own tackle.

CONTAINER

A duffle bag that will keep all your fishing gear separate from your other luggage is preferable. Having your gear separate means that it can be sent on ahead to save weight on aircraft, and similarly home again after the tour. Such a bag will hold your waders, jackets, fishing clothes and tackle boxes, and they are now made so that the rod case or cases can be strapped to the outside.

WADERS

To save weight, the new stocking-type waders are the best for travelling, and ideal for using here in the summer months. In the autumn, however, you will need thermal underwear to go with them.

Thigh waders will suffice for all South Island fishing and will also be ideal for dry-fly fishing of all North Island streams and rivers. Chest waders will be needed for lake fishing in the North Island and on some rivers like the Tongariro. So if you intend to fish in both islands, it will be essential to have both types.

CLOTHES

Essentials are rain parka, fishing jacket, hat, warm preferably-woollen socks, tennis shoes, a woollen jersey or down jacket, woollen longjohns or thermal underwear for use inside waders.

TACKLE

A torch (flashlight) is essential and, if using shooting-head line, a fold-up-type stripping basket. Fly and tackle boxes will be needed of course, not to forget Polaroid glasses.

FLY RODS

For fishing both islands, two rods are the ideal: your favourite dry-fly rod of 2.4 metres (8 ft), plus a 2.7 metre rod (9 ft) preferably weighing around 90 grams (4oz). If your budget runs to it then one of the graphite rods in either of the above lengths would suffice as one rod for both areas.

Lyndsay Taylor of Oamaru, a top salmon guide, here seen with a brown and two rainbows taken spinning on the Waitaki River in 1976

FLY LINES AND REELS

For the various types of fishing you will strike, you will need five different types of line. It is preferable to have these on five different reels, although many anglers have one reel with five interchangeable spools. Each reel or spool should have at least 200 metres of backing on it. The lines recommended are:

1. A floating line of number 6 or 7.
2. A high-density, fast-sinking line of number 8 to 10, the maximum you can handle.
3. A shooting-head line of number 10.
4. A floating line with wet or sinking tip, usually number 8.
5. A medium sinking line of number 8 to 9.

CASTS AND LEADERS

For dry-fly fishing, tapered leaders with a breaking strain of 2 kg (4–5 lb) are usual, although this depends on your preference.

For streamer flies with wet lines, anglers make up their own leaders from a roll of level monofilament of usually 2–4 kg (4–9 lb) breaking strain.

FLIES

Dry flies and nymphs are universal, so American and English patterns work equally well in New Zealand, as do the American and English pattern wet flies.

Streamer or lure flies are best purchased locally; they are available at all fishing locations and have proved themselves. However, many U.S. flies are successful here, especially Woolly Worms, Muddler Minnows and some salmon streamers.

TROLLING AND SPINNING TACKLE

For trolling, you will obviously be hiring guides with boats, and as they supply all of the tackle necessary there is no real need to bring your own. Spinning is universal, and almost any combination of rod, reel and lure used successfully at home will work equally well in New Zealand. Local favourite lures can be purchased at all fishing locations.

FISHING LICENCES

A 'tourist licence' is available only at Government Tourist bureaus and costs $4 for men and $2 for women, and is good for one month anywhere in New Zealand. Locals cannot buy this licence because of the difficulty in splitting up the $4 between the many separate acclimatisation societies; the money is given to research and for this reason the licence can only be purchased from government agencies. A normal weekly licence in any district costs $2, available at any sports store.

At the time of writing this book a universal, all-season licence is being considered and should soon become available to everyone, locals and visitors alike. It will cost approximately $10.

IMPORTATION OF TROUT FLIES AND USED FISHING TACKLE

As New Zealand is still free of some of the worst diseases affecting fowls, a serious view is taken of the importation of feathers and skins of birds from foreign lands used for the making of trout flies. The Ministry of Agriculture and Fisheries, which is responsible for fumigation of imported materials, lays down two basic rules:

1. Ready-made imported trout flies need *not* be fumigated.
2. Fly-tying materials such as loose feathers and feathers attached to skin *must* be fumigated.

Diseases in New Zealand's fisheries are also relatively unknown and to prevent the introduction of such disastrous virus diseases as VHS (viral hemorrhagic septicemia) and IPN (infectious pancreatic necrosis) the Wildlife Service of the Department of Internal Affairs appeals for the closest cooperation from visiting anglers. There are no laws preventing visitors from bringing with them their own 'used' fishing tackle such as rods, lines, reels, nets and waders. However, it is believed that disease spores from countries of known infection can be carried and transferred to other waters in such places as wader-seams, landing-net knots and felt wader soles. Visiting anglers are therefore asked to treat such items as suspect if they have had recent use in countries where diseases are known to be present. Cooperation and attention to detail of this nature will assist in keeping New Zealand disease-free and also deter possible legislation to prohibit importation of such tackle.

Salmon and trout eggs and bait from the flesh of fish are prohibited imports for the same reason, and offences of this nature are treated most seriously.

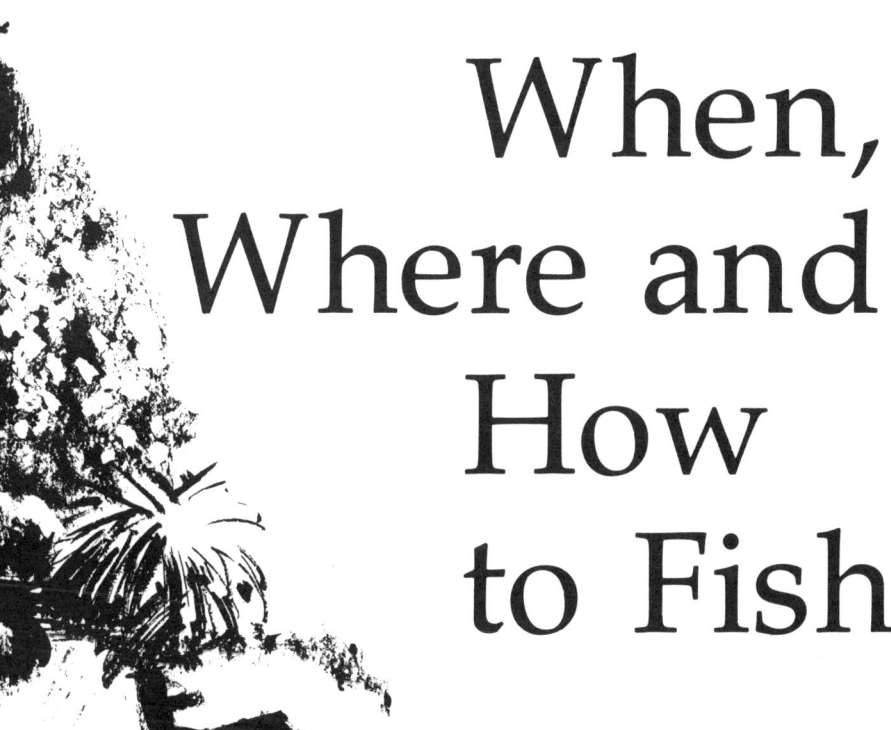

When,
Where and
How
to Fish

Almost daily I am asked questions like When should I go to such and such an area? or Where and how should I fish when I get there? The type of fishing the inquirer wishes to do is the deciding factor, because some areas are good for one method and bad for others, while all areas have their good and bad times.

At the present time there are twenty-six different acclimatisation districts in New Zealand[1] with their seasons varying from five to nine months and a few operating all year round. Some allow all methods of fishing, others don't, and many have such things as 'fly only' locations and restrictions on trolling areas. Some fish best when others are closed, and so the complexity increases. Good fishing depends on the seasons of the year, temperature of the water, weather, spawning runs and feeding habits. If the angler or guide makes a study of all these things, the picture becomes clearer and he will almost be able to set his calendar on when to go to certain areas to fish for trout, having taken most of the gamble out of the decision-making.

Lake Rotorua is shallow and in the hot summer months of January and February the water warms up considerably. Trout then gather at the spring-fed stream mouths for the colder water as well as the oxygen brought in by these streams. Be there when this seasonal change takes place and you will have excellent fishing, with limit bags a common occurrence. The same applies to fishing anywhere in the country. The mouths of the rivers emptying into the Tasman Sea in South Westland provide splendid fishing for sea-run brown trout at about the time (September) the whitebait are running. Similarly, at the mouths of the Rees and Dart rivers, Lake Wakatipu, in March, when the landlocked salmon are gathering for their spawning runs, the results can be almost a fish a cast using spinning tackle, but very much a matter of luck the rest of the season. The spawning runs in the Tongariro River at Lake Taupo almost coincide with the 'roaring' of the red stags, both brought about by a drop in temperature, so the time to go there is after Easter. So it goes on—different times for different areas for different types of fishing. I have used such knowledge in advising anglers where to go and when, and have proved time and again that if an angler is proficient at fishing the popular method for the locality concerned then the results will be almost 100 per cent successful, allowing of course for the weather being favourable.

There is a well known saying that ninety per cent of the trout are caught by ten per cent of the anglers. I don't have all the answers, as no one ever could, nor for that matter would want to, for then the

[1]See below, page 198, and accompanying maps, pages 202–3.

Tom Collins, a veteran US angler of some 24 visits, casting for trout with a dry fly on Waipunga River, central North Island

Anglers fishing the famous Red Hut pool on the legendary Tongariro River. Pool has easy access and is one of the author's favourites

Floatplane pilot Brian Brooker (in tie) flies an American client to a remote lake where he lands a trout on a fly by casting from the floats

Angling solitude on the upper Rangitaiki River, one of the North Island's fine dry-fly rivers

Ed Zern, fishing editor for Field and Stream *magazine, admires his rainbow hen taken fly casting at the Tongariro delta in 1977*

challenge would have gone out of the sport. But let's see if we can knock the odds down a little.

In designing tours for anglers, as well as guiding them, I have always used the whole country for picking locations. This obviously opens up a wide range of choices. So with that in mind let me offer a few tips that have worked well for me and may assist in taking the guesswork and gamble out of finding a location.

97

Several years ago the well known fishing guide at Turangi, Tony Jensen, phoned me to say that a storm had hit his area and the waters were unfishable. He had a client desperate for a good rainbow. Was there any water fishable at Rotorua? The same storm had also restricted things in the Rotorua area but, as it was May, I recalled that the Tarawera outlet to Lake Tarawera always ran clear in a storm and that trout would then be dropping back into the outlet to spawn. Anything was better than nothing, so Tony trailered his boat the 140 kilometres to my office, arriving at noon for directions. By a quarter to five he was back in my office, telling me the fishing was lousy but meantime edging me out to the car. Sitting in the car was my old friend Fred Goddard of Oregon with an ear-to-ear smile, and no wonder, for lying in state across the back seat was a 6.1 kg (13½ lb) fresh-run rainbow hen. They both reckoned the trip had been well worth while. That fish, incidentally, got a safe trip to Honolulu, where it now graces the wall of Fred's holiday home.

A year later I was in the same tangle. Clive Gammon, a fishing writer for the American magazine *Sports Illustrated*, had arrived at my door in the middle of a rare tropical cyclone. The same storm had ruined his fishing on the Barrier Reef in Australia, and had followed him over as if determined to spoil things here as well. Absolutely nothing was fishable at either Rotorua or Taupo; the winds had turned the lakes into seas and the rains had made the streams into rivers of silt. In desperation I phoned Tony Jensen to see if anything was fishable at Turangi. As luck would have it, there was. During excavations for the diversion tunnel between Lake Rotoaira and Tokaanu, the tunnellers had struck a huge underground stream and it was taking a massive pumping effort to discharge it into the lake. It was being pumped, crystal clear, in considerable volume down an old stream bed, the only water in the entire district not affected by the storm. Trout were gathered at the outlet like teeny-boppers around a pop star and, better still, the outlet was on the lee shore out of the hurricane winds.

Clive and I hot-footed it to Rotoaira and immediately set up our rods and began casting from the rock groin which bordered the outlet. The action became fast and furious. Clive caught his own limit and then proceeded to catch mine, all of which he returned alive to the lake. He not only got his story to justify his visit, but announced to the world in general that this was the best fishing he had experienced anywhere.

Both these examples go to prove that if you know your locations and have reliable contacts then it is not too difficult to be in the right place at the right time.

(Opposite) *Tom Collins of Missoula Montana, who has made 23 fishing trips to New Zealand, plays a trout in the Waipunga stream near the Napier-Taupo road*

A perfect example of being in the right place at the wrong time happened to me a few years back, and is offered as a suggestion of what not to do. An American TV company wanted to make a fishing film for a nationwide programm using Fabian Forte, the Hollywood actor, as the angler. The programme organiser flew out to look over locations and I showed him around the best fishing waters in the country. He liked the Tongariro River best, for the day I took him there almost every angler we saw either had a fish on the line or one on the bank. 'This', he said, 'is where we will shoot the fishing scenes.'

Three weeks later the crew of eight, including the 'star', arrived and we proceeded in convoy to Turangi, only to find the river mildly in flood and running the colour of custard, thick yellow custard. The Ministry of Works had turned New Zealand's number one noxious animals loose in the upper reaches—bulldozers. I was all for changing locations, for only a few kilometres away, at Lake Rotoaira, the water was clear and anglers were catching limit bags. But the director wouldn't wear it. He wasn't a fisherman, you see. He had been told to fish the Tongariro, so the Tongariro we fished—and we fished, and we fished, a most frustrating experience. It didn't make a very good movie. An angler has a far easier decision to make—he can switch locations to suite conditions.

In the following pages I shall deal with the reasons for going to the various types of locations at specific times. It is a guide to seasonal trout behaviour and the methods most favoured at those times.

LAKE SYSTEMS—RAINBOW TROUT

Trout living in rivers that flow to the sea will often migrate to sea for periods of up to three years, returning to the river to spawn and to live out their life span. In most of our popular lakes the trout do not have ready access to the sea, so their life style differs in that they run up the streams flowing into the lakes to spawn, returning to the lakes for the summer months. For them the lake replaces the sea.

A great deal is known about the habits of these lake-dwellers. Their pattern of life is predictable; they move to varying depths according to water temperature and food supply, factors which change with the seasons of the year.

Most lakes open for the fishing season on the first of October each year when winter spawning is over. After spawning, the trout are in very poor condition, so that when they drop back to the lake they spread out rapidly, seeking food to build up their strength. For this reason 'kelts' taken in October and November are caught by trollers, although a few stragglers will stay around the stream mouths and can be taken on a streamer fly.

The fishing is good in these months. The trout are hungry and far less choosy in their diet than maiden trout that haven't yet spawned and have remained in the lake all winter. The new arrivals will take almost anything thrown at them. They will not be as good to eat and it is a good policy to return all kelts to the water, allowing them to build up condition so that they can be fished later in the season.

There will be no great concentrations of trout anywhere, as they will have spread widely, dividing their feeding between koura and shellfish in the deeper parts and cockabullies and smelt in the shallows. Equal success will be gained by trollers using either fly lines and streamer flies on the surface or lead lines and wobbler lures at greater depths. Streamer fly at the mouths will be equally as good as fishing from the beaches with fly or spinner, or casting for cruising trout from promontories.

The seven trout with highest condition factors caught during the week-long Rotorua International fishing competition. Weights ranged from 1.8–4.5 kg (4–10 lb). All were taken from Lake Tarawera

With the warmer weather in November comes the smelt migration, and this tends to concentrate the trout into defined areas. The large schools of smelt which come to the beaches and stream mouths to spawn are often followed by large schools of trout. This period lasts from November to early January. As trout can often be seen rising all along the shoreline, it is an exciting time to go fly fishing, using floating lines and smelt-pattern flies (see section below on 'Wet-fly Fishing for Smelting Trout'). Similarly, trolling a smelt fly with a fly line in the shallows will produce far better results than trolling deep with hardware.

In the hot months of January, February and March schools of smelt are rarely found, so that trout again spread out through the lake. As the lakes warm up, trout seek out the colder water, either in the deeper layers known as thermoclines, or at the stream mouths entering the lake. Best results in these months will come from trolling, using lead or sinking fly lines to get down to these colder layers. Fly fishing also improves at the stream mouths and is usually excellent in all northern lakes. There is, however, a certain phenomenon that upsets the cold-water theory in these months. In fishing the stream mouths of Lake Taupo I have continually taken better-conditioned trout after dark than during the daylight hours. They are different fish altogether, obviously deep-water trout, much redder in the flesh and fatter. Why they should forsake the deep for the shallows at night only, I cannot say. The only explanation I can offer is that they may have sought a change of diet in moving from one cold-water layer to another. They are usually older trout and with their acquired cunning may prefer the safety of night for their foraging.

From March until the end of the season the pattern changes again. These are the months when all trout are in excellent condition, having fed well all summer in preparation for the lean winter months. Deep trolling is now better than shallow trolling, and the stream-mouth streamer-fly fishing grows interesting. Smelt will still be in evidence at the stream mouths, but the trout will not be gathering there to feed but to follow nature's love call; they will have upstream spawning on their minds. Trout have a feel for the barometer and any change of pressure heralding an approaching storm will find them congregating at the river mouths, as they need a rising river to negotiate the shallows. Thus good fly fishing will not be continuous but is often at its best just before a storm. Following the storm, most fish gathered there will have departed upstream, but another build-up then begins just before the next storm and so on. If you strike the concentrations right, you will have excellent fishing.

(Opposite) *Four attractive females, three of them from a tour party at Waihaha, Western Bay, Lake Taupo*

103

From April onwards trout will have started their upstream migrations, although some early runs will have taken place in March, depending very much on the weather. The lower pools in the river will still provide excellent fly fishing, following smelt patterns, for the trouts' feeding preferences will not have changed. Once upstream, however, feeding is not their main consideration.

Steve Rajeff of San Francisco with a typical Taupo trout taken at smelting time on the eastern shores of the lake

104

WET-FLY FISHING IN STREAMS THAT FLOW INTO LAKES

In these streams the population of trout fluctuates with the spawning runs, so there are two ways to tackle such waters. First, during summer months when only a few fish remain in the streams, and second, when the spawning runs are in full swing.

During the summer those trout remaining in the streams will respond to the same techniques as in rivers that flow to the sea. They can be taken with drys, nymphs, wets or streamer flies.

However, once the spawning runs start the situation is completely altered. These trout will be well fed and fat, fully conditioned for the long upstream journey and the strenuous love-making to follow. In fact, few eat anything at all at this time—their fat is enough to sustain them, like a bear which hibernates for the winter. They can be teased into taking a streamer fly, and most are caught when the fly passes in front of their noses, so that they either bite it from annoyance or just can't resist it. The streamers most favoured are those which imitate the food they have been fattening on in the lake they have just left, such as Parsons' Glory, Hamill's Killer, Kilwell or Mrs Simpson. Of recent years the top fly in this bracket has been the Red Setter, mainly because it looks like two trout eggs, and one thing trout *will* eat when they are spawning is another's eggs.

In my early years as a guide I regularly fished the Ngongotaha Stream flowing into Lake Rotorua and got to know it well—which really is the secret of any successful fishing anywhere. I learnt the best pools, where the fish would lie in any given pool and where to stand when making a cast. This knowledge proved invaluable when it came to taking clients there. A very fine angler from Florida, Ned Jewett, had booked me for a month's fishing tour of New Zealand, and on his very first morning in the country I took him to the Ngongotaha. It was early in the season and the river was well stocked with trout, as they hadn't all dropped back to the lake. I picked Ned up at 4.00 a.m. and drove him out to the stream where we donned waders and were ready to fish as dawn came at 5. Taking his rod from him, I tied on a Parsons' Glory, cast the fly out to a point in the river and told him to stand in that exact spot. I then pointed out an overhanging bush on the bank, told him to cast his fly just past that and allow a few seconds for it to sink before starting to retrieve. He did exactly that and made only two pulls on the line before a rainbow trout burst forth from the depths and took the fly. The fight was on.

The rainbow weighed 2.5 kg (5½ lb) and no visiting angler could ever expect a better breakfast present on his first morning in a strange country. Trouble with giving anyone an introduction like that is that

Fred Goddard of Honolulu, virtually an annual visitor to the Tongariro River, with a morning's catch of four rainbows taken from the Major Jones pool

they often expect the same result every time. But this example, like most of the fishing lessons I have learnt, proves that there is no experience like knowing your own water.

106

WET-FLY FISHING WITH SHOOTING-HEAD LINE IN STREAMS FLOWING
INTO LAKES

This method has been brought about mainly by the laws for 'fly only'
rivers, which stipulate that no weight of any form shall be attached to
fly or line. This means that to get the fly down into deep pools a
heavy, fast-sinking line is needed. It also needs light backing, which
will assist the line to sink even in a fast current. Where a normal fly
line measures 18 m (60 ft), a shooting-head line is half that length, and
the backing is usually monofilament line. The cast or leader is
generally also shorter, usually 1.2 to 1.5 m (4–5 ft), so that the fly will
not float too far above the maximum depth of the line. The angler
must be a proficient long-distance caster, because he needs to keep
not only the 9 m (30 ft) of shooting head in the air during his false
casts, but may need a final cast of up to 30 m (100 ft) on many of the big
rivers.

The procedure to cast an average 18 m (60 ft) of line is first to cast out
the shooting-head line and let it lie on the water. Then, with the line
hand, strip off another 9 m (30 ft) of monofilament from the reel and
let this lie at your feet or in your stripping basket. Next pick up the
shooting-head line in one back cast, so that on the forward or
shooting cast the weight of the shooting line will drag out the 9 m of
monofilament with it when you let go. With practice it is possible to
put out up to 30 m (100 ft) or more, although I find that every now and
then I try to handle too much line and clout myself in the back of the
head with a bunch of collapsing line.

The line is cast across the pool and the rod tip is held high after the
cast to prevent the backing from placing too much drag on the line.
The shooting head can then sink as it is being carried downstream by
the current. As the line straightens out, the fly will pass across the tail
end of the pool almost on the bottom, and theoretically in front of the
noses of any trout lying there. To cover a pool efficiently, the angler
starts at the head of the pool and after each cast takes a step
downstream so that he will work out the entire pool.

Monofilament line cannot be successfully coiled in the line hand or
held in the palm, so an alternative method must be used. I have tried
stripping in the line and allowing it to fall on the water at my feet, but
the chances are that it will be carried away by the current and place a
drag on the line, making it difficult to pick up during the next cast. I
have also observed anglers coiling the line in large loops and even
holding them in their mouths—fine for those who have mastered the
art but not everyone's kettle of oysters. The best method is to wear a
stripping basket strapped around the waist and feed the line back into
this in coils which will be easily picked up in the next cast. Some

anglers use a very light level-floating line for backing instead of monofilament. This allows a hand retrieve and does away with the need for a stripping basket.

Most trout are taken as the fly is passing across the lie, so the line hand does not have to do any retrieving except when the fly has finished its travel. Perhaps one or two strips are needed at this stage, and then the procedure is to get the line in as quickly as possible and start the next cast. The rod is usually tucked under the arm so that both hands can be used to gather the line quickly into the basket.

Once the art of handling a shooting-head line is mastered, a good angler can get his line out with only one cast instead of the four or five needed with a normal full-length line. This means that the line spends more time in the water than in the air. It is now the most popular method employed on the Tongariro River and is gaining popularity on such rivers as the Clutha, Waiau and Waitaki in the south, as well as on most salmon rivers. It can be described as the ultimate in the art of wet-fly fishing. Popular flies in conjunction with this line are the Red Setter, Partridge, Mrs Simpson, Kilwell and Hamill's Killer.

I recently had the pleasure of escorting the well known taxidermist and hunting and fishing agent, Jack Atcheson of Montana. Jack had called into New Zealand to take a quick look at the fishing he had heard so much about and see for himself whether it would be worth persuading clients to travel here. He had only two days to spend, one to fish and the other to look at hotels and sights.

As for fishing, I knew there was only one place offering trout at this time—the Tongariro. I drove him there but gave the river very little build up. I was rather apprehensive, wondering whether Jack could use a shooting-head line, for if he couldn't he wasn't going to catch any fish. I should not have worried.

We arrived at the Major Jones pool to find my old friend Fred Goddard of Honolulu already ensconced in the water with four fresh-run rainbows on the bank and, I might add, a very satisfied smile on his face. Tony Jensen was waiting for us with a rod and line all set up with his favourite Red Setter fly so that there would be no wasted fishing time. Fred waved Jack in ahead of him, a fine sporting gesture, as anglers have an unwritten law that you should take your place behind someone already working a pool. Tony Jensen gave Jack the rundown on a shooting-head line and the lie of the pool and left him to it. His second cast latched him on to a fine rainbow which spent most of its time above the surface dancing on its tail—a great excuse to break out the cameras and coffee. His fourth cast after coffee produced another, whereupon Jack wound in his line and said, 'Now

I know the fishing is good. I don't need any more—won't be able to eat what I've already caught. Let's go.' Possibly with his future clients in mind, Jack wasn't going to exhaust our fishery!

LAKE FISHING WITH WET FLY

During the summer when trout have returned to the lakes after spawning, there are two types of fishing available according to the depth of the lake. Most lakes warm up in the summer so that trout in the deeper ones will seek lower thermoclines and in the shallow lakes seek the colder temperatures brought in by spring-fed streams. The two types of lake are fished differently.

In shallow lakes there will often be large concentrations of trout

A fine fish taken on a dry fly from the Oreti River, Southland. Successful angler is Walton Powell, a Californian rod-maker, and looking on is actor, William Conrad, famous for his TV role as 'Cannon'

gathered at the stream mouths and this makes for excellent wet-fly fishing. Sinking lines are the most commonly used, but whenever surface activity is observed floating lines may prove equally productive. There will invariably be a lip or drop-off into deeper water where the current of the stream meets the breaking waves of the lake and trout prefer to lie behind this lip. I like to stand well back from the lip so as not to be seen by the trout. A long cast will get the fly out past the lip, so that on the retrieve it will pass along the bottom and over the lip, getting as close to the trout as possible. It is quite common to get a strike when you thus have a handful of line. I usually drop it on to the water at my feet and let the line run out through the fingers until it is all back on the reel.

For daytime fishing, smelt flies such as Grey Ghost, Parsons' Glory, Taupo Tiger or Hamill's Killer are most popular.

These stream mouths also fish exceptionally well at night. The fishing method remains the same, except that night-time flies are used such as Craig's Night, Ewe Wasp, Hairy Dog or Black Phantom. A little care is needed with night fishing to avoid two common problems. When retrieving the line in the dark make sure you don't pull the line-to-leader knot into the rod-tip guide or tangles will ensue on the next cast. You must also watch that the tail on the fly is not too long as at night it is common to get this tail caught around the hook. I check mine every other cast to make sure that I am not fishing with a dead fly.

In deep lakes there will not as a rule be any large concentrations of trout found around stream mouths except when they are gathering to run. Wet-fly fishing on such lakes during the summer is therefore mainly confined to cruising trout. For cruisers, anglers wear polaroid glasses and stand either on rocky promontories or out from the shore on the edge of a drop-off where the trout can be spotted as they swim past. This method, of course, can be used on almost any lake. It is popular in the South Island and also at Lake Waikaremoana. A variation is to drift in a boat along a shoreline or across shallow reefs, casting blindly or for a specific trout. The best flies for this type of angling are Parsons' Glory, Grey Ghost, Hamill's Killer or any of the smelt pattern.

WET-FLY FISHING FOR SMELTING TROUT IN LAKES

Where lakes have an abundant population of smelt, these come into the beaches and stream mouths to spawn, usually from early November to early January. They will be evident in thick schools all along the beaches and at, or just inside, the stream mouths. Trout follow these schools into the shallows and can be observed ripping through them in a feeding frenzy. I have often seen the water literally boiling. In most cases the trout come up fast from below and take the smelt just beneath the surface, the speed of the strike often carrying the attacker out of the water in what is known as a 'rise'. I have seen trout almost beach themselves in their enthusiasm for the chase. At other times the trout will only swirl near the surface as it takes the smelt.

These months when trout are smelting are an exciting time to go fishing. It is summer, the water is warm, and one can wade along the shore in tennis shoes and shorts. I prefer a floating line and seldom use anything other than a Grey Ghost fly, occasionally a Parson's Glory. Seldom do I wade out further than up to my knees and in many cases cast from the beach itself.

I like to cast for specific rises, or just cast out and let the line float on the surface, so that, if a trout rises near by, it only takes one back and one forward cast to put the fly over the rise. It is as near to dry-fly fishing as one can get, for in many cases you will be able to watch the trout take the fly.

Using a floating line, there is no need to coil or palm the retrieved line. I just let it drop on the surface of the water at my feet, for it will not drift away as in a river current. The line is retrieved very fast, often as fast as one can go, simulating the speed of an escaping smelt in spurts of 150–300 mm (6–12 inches). I also like to pause occasionally during the retrieve, as this will often make a trout strike if he thinks the smelt is tiring. I learnt this one day when casting from the back of Ron Houghton's anchored launch in Western Bay, Lake Taupo. The water was gin clear, and on several casts I observed a trout following the fly almost up to the boat or until it spotted me, when it would dart away. The trout may suspect that the smelt is artificial and may be following it out of curiosity, so a pause in the retrieve will often fool him long enough to result in a strike.

My son Roger and I were fishing one day for smelting trout on Lake Taupo. We had boiled the billy and had a trout smoking in the cooker for lunch. We were lying on the beach less than a metre from the water's edge polishing off a couple of cans of 'hop sandwich', when a trout rose for a smelt right beside us. It almost beached itself and splashed us with water before turning to swim quietly away through the shallows. Roger reached for his rod and made a quick cast from the horizontal position. Amazingly, he hooked the trout, the only one I ever saw taken lying down.

Another time in Western Bay, Ron Houghton, the patriarch of Taupo guides, and I made ourselves some 'fishing to order'. I had taken a client on a thirty-day safari around New Zealand and returned from the South Island ahead of schedule with a full bag of trophies and time up my sleeve. I therefore engaged Ron and his overnight charter launch *Mananui* to take us to Waihaha Stream for a few days' fishing. It was a summer weekend and unfortunately there were campers and anglers at all the best stream mouths for fly fishing. This would normally not have been a problem, but my client could not cast too well and was reluctant to fish alongside experienced long-distance casters.

We had therefore to find some quiet place for him, preferably one we could have all to ourselves. Ron suggested Chinamans Creek, a small stream where no one was fishing because a prolonged easterly wind had changed its course at the mouth so that it ran alongside the lake and flowed out through a rockery. We had shovels on the boat and reckoned that if we dug the stream straight out into its old course, we could create a rip that would attract trout. I told the client what we were going to do but he just laughed and I doubt if he understood what I was talking about. Ron and I stripped off our shirts and, taking a shovel each, set to with a will and dug solidly for three hours. All of this time the American took still photos and movies of us toiling away. I am sure he thought it a great joke and that we were completely off our rockers—he almost had us convinced we were.

By dark, however, the stream was flowing straight out into the lake with a good swift current for some twenty metres. We cleaned up for dinner and decided not to start fishing until 8.00 p.m. or later, which would give the trout a chance to come in from the deep water. After dark the odd plop could be heard out in the rip to prove the fish were there and we took up our positions with a Black Phantom fly on each line. The client was placed in the centre of the rip to take advantage of the current to get his line out, and Ron and I stationed ourselves on either side of him.

Zap! Ron took a fish on his first cast and I took one on my second, both beautiful silver deep-water rainbows for which Taupo is famous. We played and unhooked them, then walked back to our positions and promptly took another each. The third time it happened the same way. It was becoming decidedly embarrassing, for my client hadn't yet hooked one. We swapped rods with him, places with him and offered him our fish to play after they were hooked—all to no avail. One thing about him—he was a sportsman, determined to catch his own fish. Ron and I carried on and caught five or six trout each but felt so lousy doing so we finally packed up. Our partner hadn't caught a thing. He persevered for a little while longer then gave up in disgust.

Angler shows size of two 4 kg Rangitikei rainbows which were later flown out by helicopter to be mounted for display

Author fishing on the Tahuna-a-tara River, Atiamuri, North Island. A beautiful wet-fly stream with results shown in the foreground

The Tongariro is perhaps one of the most heavily fished in New Zealand, plus one of the most prolific. Here an angler lands one of the many thousands of trout caught annually in this river

Mrs Waterman, wife of well-known American fishing writer Charles Waterman, hooks a trout while fishing a nymp on Lake Otomangakau, central North Island.

I happen to know that when that chap returned home he took some casting lessons. Trout fishing at night, a favourite pastime for local anglers, is not popular with overseas guests. It is something they have never been used to. This is one reason why most guides keep strictly to daytime fishing. It is harder work fishing by day but it probably makes better fishermen of them.

One morning I will always remember saw me escorting an American TV team around New Zealand. They had agreed to make five trout-fishing movies in the country and I was commissioned to arrange the tour and take them to the right places. Ed Sierer, an expert fly fisherman who ran a weekly TV programme on fishing in Seattle, was the front man and leader of the group. We left the launching ramp at Tokaanu before daylight that morning so as to be at the Tongariro River by 5.00 a.m., where we would wait for the sun to rise before we started filming. The camera was equipped with magnetic sound so that all the actors wore microphones. Our boats anchored about two metres apart and as the sun came up, so did the trout. It was absolutely incredible. There were four of us fishing and at times we had four rainbows on at once. The sound track was full of screaming reels and good old Kiwi adjectives. Ed Sierer netted two fish at once and described it as the best fishing he had ever experienced anywhere. Proof of this was that in two hours we had completed one full half-hour programme. The other four took between two and four days each to complete.

TROLLING ON LAKES

Where to fish on a lake and how deep are the major decisions one has to make—decisions that will mean the success or failure of an outing.

Sail out on to a lake for the first time to find you are all alone on the lake—a common occurrence in this country—and you will be in trouble. You won't know where to start. But go out on to a lake where many other boats are fishing and your decision will be made for you. People gravitate to each other. They are generally in a certain place for a good reason—trout are schooled-up there or it's a proved feeding ground.

I have never been one for fishing in a crowd and prefer quiet spots, and a little research into why fish are in certain areas and at certain depths can be most rewarding.

Not long ago I took my two sons to Taupo for a few days' fishing and we headed the launch for Western Bay, where we found in one bay that trout were rising all along the shoreline. We paid out fly lines and used my old favourite, the Parsons' Glory fly. The trout were obviously rising for smelt. We had the bay to ourselves and by trolling about fifty metres out from the shore in shallow water were soon picking up a great many trout.

Another boat then turned up. When its occupants saw that we were having success they came in close to follow our course—you couldn't altogether blame them for wanting to be in on the action. But even as we watched they stopped dead three times and seemed to be having all sorts of bother. Finally they decided to draw alongside and ask us what we were using, and could not believe it when we told them fly lines and flies. They had been using lead lines and three of them had been lost, snagged on the bottom—a very expensive morning for them. Altogether a very good lesson in not following others blindly but applying some common sense to each situation as it arises.

The majority of trout taken by trollers come from lake bottoms as the lure passes just above feeding beds, across a submerged reef, or over a favourite hole. Those few taken at intermediate depths will most likely be occupying a temporary thermocline or layer of water at a preferred temperature or they may be cruising a beat along the base of cliffs. Other exceptions to the depth rule are annual phenomena like the green beetle hatch or when schools of smelt are available on the surface; at these times trout can be taken very successfully by trolling with floating or shallow lines. When trout are taking smelt they will often be observed rising out of the water or swirling on the surface. During the beetle hatch myriads of beetles will sometimes form great rafts on the surface, yet one will see few rises. If you watch these rafts closely, you may see trout just breaking the surface with their noses as they pluck the beetles from below. A small green streamer fly for beetles and Grey Ghost streamer for smelting trout will be ideal in such situations, attached to a floating line. But if there is no visible surface activity then, like the devil, down you will have to go for action, and in general you will find more activity close to the bottom than you will at intermediate levels. I like to get my lines as near to the bottom as possible because, obviously, if the trout are down deep that's where they will be feeding. The correct depth is more important than the right lure, which is why depth-finders are having such a boom in popularity. It is now also possible to purchase temperature recorders which give the temperature at any given depth. A combination of the two is lethal. They certainly take the guesswork out of trolling—and for most of us, I guess, the fun too. I enjoy my fishing without using either.

BROWN TROUT IN LAKES

Browns are not as susceptible to change in water temperature as rainbows and as a rule each species prefers a different type of water within the lake. Brown trout, however, are not consistent in their behaviour and those in South Island lakes live differently from those in North Island lakes. The difference is so marked that it has even been suggested they might be different subspecies. But a *Salmo trutta* is still a *Salmo trutta* whether living north, south or half way up the Volga.

The difference between the North Island and South Island brown is mainly one of environment. The southern lakes are snow fed and much colder than the northern ones and therefore do not carry the same abundance of plankton and small fish life such as smelt, bullies, shellfish and freshwater crayfish. Browns can be taken in the southern lakes on a dry fly and many are caught by trolling, whereas in the north it is almost impossible to take one on a dry fly and seldom are they caught when trolling. The southern browns appear to feed more on surface insects and hatches, and because of the lack of an abundant small fish life will readily take a trolled lure or spinner; they live, in fact, more like rainbows. In the north, on the contrary, they live so well that they seem to spurn a troller's efforts, and are rarely taken on a streamer fly at a stream mouth. Indeed I have never taken one on a smelt fly when rainbows have been most active attacking schools of smelt. Altogether, when fishing for rainbows by the popular methods, one will seldom chance on a brown in the north. So difficult are they to take, that the Wildlife authorities have taken off all limits on browns in both Lake Rotorua and Lake Taupo.

In the clear southern lakes the most popular method of fishing for browns is to don polaroid glasses and watch for cruising fish, then cast a fly or lure ahead of them. This is seldom possible in the northern lakes. The majority of browns taken there are caught at night using large black-bodied streamer flies usually in the slack water or eddies off to either side of a stream mouth. These flies imitate freshwater crayfish or bullies.

I learnt a great deal about brown trout as a young ranger based at Rotorua when I was told to catch live browns to replace dwindling stocks in some of the trout springs. I took a long-handled net and torch and went to a long shallow beach one night after eleven o'clock, not wanting to alarm law-abiding citizens who might think I was poaching, which I was . . . legally. I waded along up to my knees in the water, shining the torch ahead of me, and what I learnt that first night was a revelation. Rainbows swimming into the light—and there were lots of them—would take off at burnt-rubber speed like Denny Hulme at the drop of a flag, but browns would take no notice of the light whatsoever. They would just keep right on swimming lazily towards me, and if I kept the torch ahead of me, and above and ahead of the net, they would swim ever so casually straight into it. On any still night that I went to the lake I saw literally hundreds of browns cruising the shallows, more than I would ever have thought possible, and it certainly gave me encouragement to fish for them.

Quite by accident I also discovered the browns' fondness for mice. When another ranger and I were cleaning out the pheasant pens at the game farm, we found a nest of baby mice and promptly placed them in a preserving jar with the intention of trying them out on the big hungry browns of Lake Rotorua. We had a lot of fun preparing the attack and decided to use bare hooks to which we would attach a live mouse using a rubber band. The results were deadly and we had an exciting night's fishing, although of course we had to pay the line out gently. Any attempt at an energetic cast would have propelled the mouse into space like a Cape Kennedy rocket. This method is legal in some districts.

Browns appear to establish their own territories, much the same as a Sika stag, and maintain a beat up and down a given area, often remaining in the same location year after year. The bigger and older they become, the wiser they are. Big browns are not easy to catch in northern lakes, but some of the difficulties will be removed if the angler realises that it requires a different method to that used for rainbows.

FISHING RIVERS THAT FLOW TO THE SEA

Trout living in these rivers are known as 'resident fish', for although they have no lakes to migrate to, both rainbows and browns will on occasion migrate to sea for a period and then return to the river to complete their life span. The biggest migration of sea-run browns takes place in South Westland; others occur in Southland and in the east coast rivers of Canterbury. Sea runs of either rainbows or browns are apparently not so common in the North Island, though little research has been done on the subject. However, I have spoken to commercial fishermen who have picked up both rainbows and browns in their nets off Wairoa mouth in Hawke's Bay and off the Whakatane River mouth in the Bay of Plenty. Much research remains to be done in all rivers of both islands.

The feeding pattern of river trout remains fairly constant all year round, except for the insect breeding cycles which peak at various times and the boost in diet which occurs when whitebait are running. Whitebait migrate from the sea up most rivers flowing into it, usually in September and October. To take advantage of this bonanza, South Westland opens its trout-fishing season on 1 September, while in other West Coast districts further north many of the rivers are also open to fishing in the sections between the road bridges and sea. Good numbers of trout follow the whitebait in from the sea, while resident fish in the lower reaches also congregate for this desirable food, just as they school together in pursuit of smelt in lakes. This is therefore an exciting time to go fishing in all those areas where it is permitted, using smelt-pattern streamer flies or spinning gear with silver smelt-imitation spinners.

Apart from this bonus supplement to the trout's diet, the normal pattern of river life in the middle and upper reaches is predictable, with trout feeding much the same all year round, whether the rivers are clear and shallow or dark and deep.

Where rainbows and browns share the same river they do tend to keep apart, with the browns preferring pools and the rainbows more likely to be found in the rippled water between pools. In those larger rivers that have many small side streams flowing into them the seasonal pattern will be much the same as in lakes, for these side streams will be the preferred spawning streams and there will be migrations from big to small, and therefore concentrations of trout at these stream mouths prior to spawning.

All these rivers experience an early morning and evening rise during the summer months when hatches of insects are taking place. This is the favoured feeding time for trout and they can then be tempted with imitation dry flies. During this rise trout will be more active in the pools and can be seen circling on the watch for larvae rising or insect life on the surface. In the middle of the day, however, they are more likely to be resting at the edge of the pool, and will often lie so still that one has to look hard to detect any fin movement. When they are in this resting phase, they are most difficult to catch, although a persistent angler can sometimes tease them into striking, if a lure is passed almost across their nose.

On shallow streams a floating line with a sinking tip is ideal, but on deeper streams one should use a medium to high density sinking line, depending on the depth required. The best results with wet flies are achieved by presenting the fly sideways across the pool so that the line swings across and down to the tail end of the pool where most trout will be lying in wait. It is also a good plan to work out the rippled water between pools, as in this water they will readily take a wet fly. If trout are cruising around at the head of the pool, they will be more interested in dry-fly or nymph presentations.

In the bigger, darker and deeper rivers trout live the same daily life pattern, with the difference that these rivers have an abundant additional food supply such as koura (freshwater crayfish), frogs and tadpoles. These are therefore preferred spinning rivers, using spinners that imitate those creatures. Though these big rivers are often dark and mysterious, they can provide excellent fishing if one uses dry fly morning and evening and spinners or wet fly during the day.

To sum up, rivers that flow to the sea fish best early and late in the season with wet fly or spinners, and best with dry fly during the hot summer months when insect hatches are evident.

CAUTION WHEN STALKING TROUT

Stalking trout is half the fun of river fishing. Remember when you went rabbit shooting? If you thumped your feet above a bank, every rabbit within a hundred metres would be diving down a burrow. The same happens with trout. They can both see and hear you, especially near those clear shallow dry-fly streams. They are also shy of the shadow of a line passing over them and of a line landing on the water with a splash.

On occasion I have seen anglers approach a stream on their hands and knees, others casting from so far back as to be almost out of sight of the pool. Extreme cases, no doubt, but it certainly pays to remember that if a trout is startled by sight or sound it will be almost impossible to catch.

BEST TIMES TO GO FISHING

Trout fishing remains primarily an individual sport and in time every angler will build up his own store of knowledge concerning favourite fishing waters. Keeping a diary helps in this regard—even a simple record of places, weather conditions and methods used. It is all too easy to forget such details. Highly successful outings will doubtless stick in the mind but confusion is almost bound to arise over outings with limited success, however pleasurable in themselves.

In advising anglers where and when to go no writer can hope to take account of particular local conditions such as when spring tides will free the outlet to the Waituna Lagoon in Southland or when there has been a fresh in the Canterbury rivers causing the salmon to run. Similarly those fishermen living near hydro dams will have knowledge of when the turbines are switched on and off. These purely local effects are found in every fishing area in the country and it sometimes pays dividends to ask a few questions beforehand of the locals. I prefer that kind of assurance when travelling to another district and usually phone a friend in the area. Failing that, more often than not the local sports store will have some helpful information.

CALENDAR OF POPULAR LOCATIONS

SEPTEMBER Opening of fishing South Westland/Fiordland for sea-run brown trout.

OCTOBER Opening of most lakes, some streams and rivers in all districts. Good trolling month.

NOVEMBER Smelting starting in all lakes. Wet fly and harling excellent. Start of good dry-fly hatches. Dry-fly fishing good on all streams open.

DECEMBER Opening of streams flowing into lakes—fishing these streams excellent. Smelting in progress on lakes. Good wet fly and harling. Good wet and dry on all streams.

JANUARY Last month for smelting trout. Excellent wet-fly fishing at stream mouths, especially Rotorua and Taupo. Good trolling month with fly lines, streamer fly. Holidaymakers make dry-fly fishing on popular streams difficult.

FEBRUARY Stream-mouth fishing; streamer fly in lakes is excellent. Most holidaymakers gone home. Dry fly on streams excellent. Trolling good everywhere, although switching to deeper lines. Salmon runs starting in Canterbury rivers.

MARCH Trout beginning to gather at stream mouths. Last good month for dry-fly fishing on streams. Good night fishing northern lakes at stream mouths. Good salmon fishing in Canterbury rivers. Good stream-mouth fishing in southern lakes for landlocked salmon.

APRIL Last month of season in many districts. Stream mouths provide best fishing. Especially good at Lake Taupo. Good month for spinning everywhere. Runs starting in Tongariro River.

MAY Big rainbows gathering at stream mouths in Lake Tarawera. Spawning runs excellent in Taupo rivers. Good stream-mouth fishing southern lakes.

JUNE Last month of season in all districts. Excellent stream-mouth streamer fly in all lakes. Excellent on Tongariro River.

Parts of New Zealand remain open all winter as follows:

JULY TO AUGUST Good river fishing Tongariro and Tauranga-Taupo rivers at Taupo. Good trolling in Lakes Rotorua and Taupo, in Lake Benmore and in Waikato hydro lakes.

North Island Trout Fishing Locations

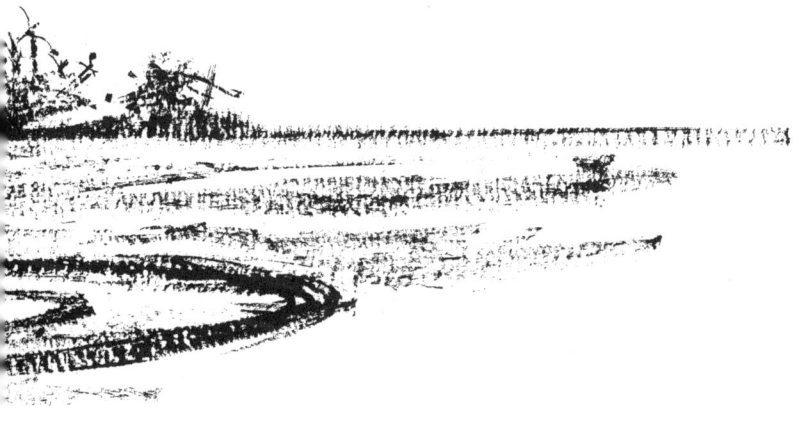

In writing about the trout fishing to be found in the North Island it is natural to deal first with the Rotorua-Taupo lake system. This is the one general location made famous for more than fifty years by anglers from all over the world, mainly because the fishing is accessible, relatively easy and guides have been and still are readily available. It is understandable that visitors and locals alike should have devoted their time and attention to this broad area, largely to the exclusion of the rest of the North Island.

Any continuation of this exclusiveness would, I feel, be a mistake. By all means make the most of Rotorua-Taupo but it is high time that the quite fabulous fishing available in other parts of the North Island became better known. For instance, dry-fly fishing areas in the Waikato, the Wairarapa, Hawke's Bay and the Bay of Plenty certainly rival anything to be found in the South Island. Similarly the remote reaches of the Wanganui, Rangitikei, Mohaka and Wairoa rivers with their tributary systems produce some of the best fishing in New Zealand.

This chapter sets out to describe these locations, including of course Rotorua-Taupo, and to offer a little advice on suitable methods of fishing them. Flies and lures are largely a matter of personal choice and seasonal variation but some suggestions have been included.

In selecting areas only those known to be productive are dealt with, though any number of other areas are known to contain trout. The named locations will at least provide starting points for forays farther afield. If someone's favourite location is not mentioned, there may be consolation in the fact that it will remain comparatively undisturbed. Personally I am not a fan of those locations that provide standing room only. I much prefer quiet pastures and for those who feel the same it is to be hoped that there will be some value in the following suggestions.

I have chosen to ignore acclimatisation district boundaries and deal rather with individual lakes or entire river systems or watersheds. One reason for this is that such general locations will remain constant, whereas district boundaries may well be changed if acclimatisation societies amalgamate.

Availability of Guides. In the North Island guiding activity is concentrated on the Rotorua-Taupo lake region, with operators working from their headquarters in Rotorua city and the Taupo lakeside towns of Taupo, Tokaanu and Turangi. All guides have boats and all necessary tackle, so that the client can arrive in his best Sunday clothes and be completely outfitted for a trip. Eighty per cent of the guides are trollers who are expert in this type of fishing but know little about fly fishing. The other twenty per cent are expert streamer-fly anglers who really dislike trolling but are always willing to do it to fill out their working season. For dry-fly fishing, there are several guides prepared and equipped to drive to outlying streams within a day's reach of their headquarters.

Short-term visitors will find that all guides have their cards with contact phone numbers prominently displayed in hotels and motels. Alternatively the Government Tourist Bureau and municipal public relations offices can arrange suitable contacts. These organisations also welcome inquiries by mail. One company, Trout Fishing Consultants, P.O. Box 2204, Rotorua, arranges trout-fishing tours anywhere in New Zealand.

ROTORUA LAKES

There are ten fishable lakes within a 30-km radius of Rotorua city, which are dealt with below in the following order: Rotorua, Tarawera, Okataina, Rotoiti, Rotoma, Rotoehu, Rerewhakaaitu, Rotomahana, Okareka and Tikitapu (Blue Lake). All contain rainbow trout, but browns are found only in Rotorua and Rotoiti. The average trout caught weighs 0.9–1.4 kg (2–3 lb) but trout in the 2.3–2.7 class (5–6 lb) are caught regularly. An exception is Lake Tarawera, where trout have been averaging 1.8–2.3 kg (4–5 lb) in recent seasons, with trout in the 4.1–5.0 kg class (9–12 lb) appearing late in the season. Very little spinning is done, but trolling is most popular and productive on all of the lakes. Wet-fly fishing at stream mouths using sinking lines is the most productive fly-fishing method, with streamer flies used almost exclusively.

Lake Rotorua. This is the greatest fish producer of all the Rotorua lakes, the fish being predominantly rainbows averaging 0.9–1.4 kg (2–3 lb). Every week fish of 2.3–2.7 kg (5–6 lb) are taken, and others over 3.2 kg (7 lb) show up during the season. It is a shallow lake (maximum depth 26 metres) with safe wading at all stream mouths, and is the only lake in the district which is open to fishing all year round. It has both rainbow and brown trout, but the rainbows predominate. Trolling is constant all year round. Being shallow, the lines most favoured are fly lines trolled with either streamer flies or spoons. Normally the trolling is best 300 metres off the stream mouths, or elsewhere around 200 metres off shore.

The streamer-fly fishing is best in the summer months when the lake warms up and the trout gather in large concentrations at the stream mouths for the cold water and oxygen brought in by various spring-fed streams. Limit bags are common at this time (usually January and February), especially at the mouths of the Awahou,

Mel Kreiger from San Francisco, well known outdoors travel agent, with his wife Fanny, poses with his first trout taken in New Zealand from Lake Tarawera in 1968

Hamurana and Waiteti. Otherwise all stream mouths, including the above as well as the Ngongotaha, Utuhina and Ohau Channel, fish well early and late in the season, when fish are either dropping back out of the feeder streams or gathering to run up to spawn.

In January 1976 a 13-year-old schoolboy, Lance Moana, caught a 6.5 kg (14 lb 6 oz) brown trout in the lower Ngongotaha Stream, which will give an idea of the type of trout that are available.

Best of the feeder streams are the Ngongotaha and Waiteti, which open upstream from the lake on 1 December. These fish well during the month of December when fish are dropping back to the lake, but are almost devoid of fish during the summer, with runs starting again usually in May and June when they again fish exceptionally well.

Trolling is best done with fly lines and streamer flies as used in fly fishing. Favoured spoons are the Toby, Flamingo, Penny, Mother of Pearl, Zed Spinner and Billy Hill. Favoured streamer flies for streams, lakes and harling are Grey Ghost, Parsons' Glory, Hamill's Killer, Kilwell, Lord's Killer—all most favoured during daylight hours. Stream mouths fish better after dark and at these times darker flies such as Craig's Night, Ewe Wasp, Taihape Tickler and Hairy Dog are recommended.

124

Lake Tarawera. While Rotorua produces the most fish, Tarawera is not so well endowed, and many is the day spent on it for no fish. But it can be most rewarding when one is successful, as the trout run anything from 1.3-2.26 kg (3-5 lb). There are no browns in this lake.

It is a very deep clear lake, and even from the beginning of the season few trout will be taken on a fly. It is towards the end of the season (May and June), when trout begin to gather at the stream mouths before running up to spawn, that most fly fishing is done. So from the start of the season until May the majority of trout are taken trolling, and because the fish are deep in lower thermoclines most are taken on lead or wire lines. There are exceptions. I know one guide who has great success harling fly lines with streamer flies, and the same chap also takes the odd fish fly-fishing over shallow shoals during the summer. But his is a rare case.

Fly fishing at the end of the season is mainly concentrated at the three main entering spawning streams, Te Wairoa, Wairua and Waitangi, and at the lake outlet—the beginning of the Tarawera River. All these locations are fished heavily from 5.00 a.m. until 11.00 p.m., with the greatest concentration of anglers arriving usually at dark and fishing until closing, which will give an idea of when most trout are taken, but these stream mouths are becoming very overcrowded.

The Wairua and Waitangi streams have lake access only, so that anglers need boats to reach both mouths. Te Wairoa Stream can be reached by car from Rotorua and the outlet of the Tarawera River is reached by car from Kawerau.

Most popular flies, all streamers, are Kilwell, Mrs Simpson, Hamill's Killer, Craig's Night, Ewe Wasp, Hairy Dog and Black Phantom. As for trolling lures, the Cobra would be number one on this lake in both small and large size and preferably green. Next would be the large Toby in green and black, the Flatfish and Pearl on brass, and Mother of Pearl.

The biggest trout taken in 1977 was a 5.45-kg (12 lb) rainbow by Mr T. Rotarangi on a fly at the mouth of Te Wairoa Stream. The biggest recorded in recent times was a 8.61-kg (19 lb) rainbow, taken in May 1957 by Perry Preston.

Lake Okataina. This lake is completely surrounded by scenic reserve and is reached along a single road, so that access to all bays and beaches is by boat from the lodge area at road end. The fishing is predominantly trolling, although there is some good fly fishing available late in the season, April to June, in such places as the Log Pool, the Dogger Bank and along the beach in front of the lodge. Trolling is mainly successful with lead lines out from 50 to 100 metres, and best lures are Cobra, Toby, Flatfish and Penny. Trolling a streamer fly is also successful in the summer months, especially smelt flies such as Grey Ghost, Taupo Tiger, Hamill's Killer and Kilwell.

Trout here are all rainbows and run an average of 0.9–1.4 kg (2–3 lb). As a point of interest, this is the only lake where I have ever caught a trout using a rapala. Overseas anglers had told me how good the rapala was, so I sent for a couple. Some time later I was out on Okataina with Allan Beamish-White, the top guide in the area at the time, and the fishing was exceptionally tough. Getting down to the bottom of my tackle box, I found a rapala still in its plastic box and tied it on to the leader much to Allan's amusement, as the look on his face said, 'You'll never catch nothing on that.' I had hardly paid out the line when—zam!—a rainbow literally screamed line from the reel. When I got it to net, it turned out to be a nice fat 2.3-kg (5-lb) hen. I tried the rapala out in various lakes with much enthusiasm from that day on, but have yet to catch another trout on it. It obviously does not suit New Zealand conditions.

A tour party fishing one of the best rips on Lake Taupo, that at the influx of the Waihaha Stream, Western Bay. The author's boat, Sheez-Rite, *helped to transport the anglers, access being by water only*

NORTH ISLAND TROUT FISHING LOCATIONS

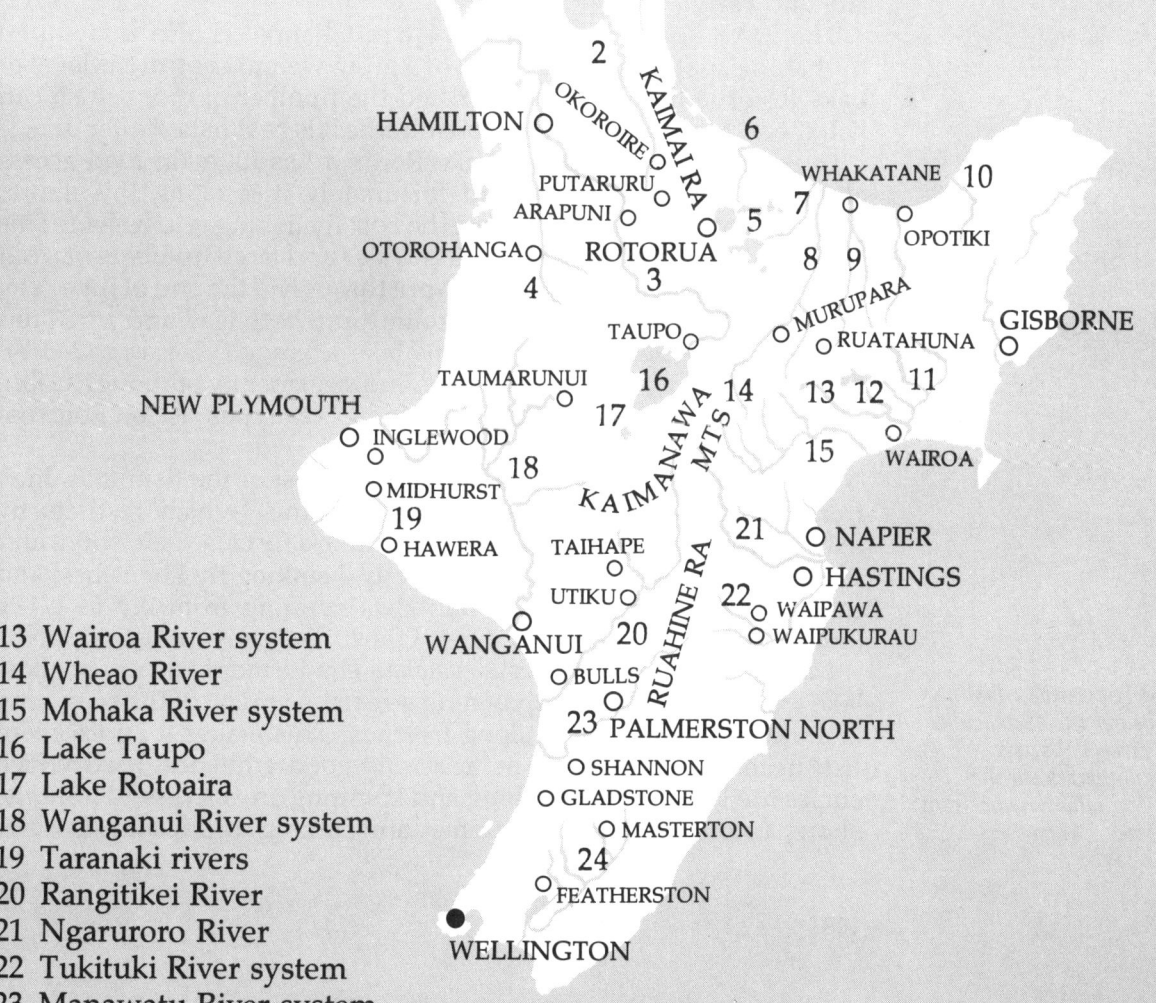

 1 Wairoa River system and Kai Iwi Lakes
 2 Waihou River system
 3 Waikato River and hydro lakes
 4 Waipa River system
 5 Rotorua lakes
 6 Kaituna River
 7 Tarawera River
 8 Rangitaiki River
 9 Whakatane River system
10 Motu River
11 Ruakituri River system
12 Lakes Waikaremoana and Waikare-iti

13 Wairoa River system
14 Wheao River
15 Mohaka River system
16 Lake Taupo
17 Lake Rotoaira
18 Wanganui River system
19 Taranaki rivers
20 Rangitikei River
21 Ngaruroro River
22 Tukituki River system
23 Manawatu River system
24 Ruamahanga River system and Lake Wairarapa

Lake Rotoiti and the Ohau Channel. This lake, connected to Lake Rotorua by the Ohau Channel, has both rainbow and brown trout. Because it has limited spawning streams, the main fishing done on Rotoiti is trolling, and mainly with fly lines since lead lines are prohibited. Because of the restricted spawning, most trout travel through the Ohau Channel to the streams entering Rotorua where they do their spawning. The Ohau Channel thus provides excellent fly fishing early and late in the season, as it is then the trout are travelling to or from spawning.

Trolling is good anywhere in the lake but more especially at the eastern end on both the north and south sides, the latter depending on wind direction.

Fly fishing is good off the wharf at Okere, at the outlet of the Ohau Channel and off the beach at Ruato Bay, all of which can be reached by road. The best stream mouth is the Waiiti, which can be waded but is best fished from a boat. As with all fly fishing in the district, it is best late and early.

The Lake Rotorua end of the Ohau Channel is also a favoured fly-fishing spot, but the building of a groin weir to control the level of Lake Rotorua has severely restricted the number of rods which can fish there. Moreover, to avoid boat traffic it is best fished after dark.

Lakes Rotoma and Rotoehu. Lake Rotoma has its main road access along the southern shore and fortunately it is along this shore, especially on Oneroa Beach, that the best fly fishing is to be had. This beach provides the main spawning water and large numbers of trout can be seen in the shallows from April through to the end of June. The rest of the lake provides mainly trolling and both lead and wire lines can be used. The rainbows in this lake average 0.9–1.4 kg (2–3 lb). Trolling is best with sinking fly lines and streamer fly, although Cobra and Pearl are both successful—streamer-fly types as for Rotorua, Rotoiti and Tarawera.

Lake Rotoehu has little road access, so most of the fishing is done from boats. There are few entering streams, which restricts fly fishing, and most fishing is done by trolling a fly close in to shore and up and down the various arms. Mainly a sinking fly line is best and the trout are predominantly rainbows running from 0.9 to 1.4 kg (2–3 lb). Parsons' Glory and Grey Ghost flies prove most popular.

Lakes Rerewhakaaitu and Rotomahana. The former is a very shallow lake with really only one spawning stream, so much of the spawning is done in shallow water along beaches. This makes it an excellent fish-from-the-shore lake, as access is good from the road which circles the lake. Both fly fishing and spinning are successful from the shore, and trolling is best with medium sinking fly line and streamer

(Opposite) *Fishing below the spectacular Tieke Falls, six kilometres up the Waihaha Stream from Lake Taupo*

fly. Most popular fly fishing is on the Homestead Arm. Best flies are Hamill's Killer, Kilwell, Mrs Simpson and the smelt patterns such as Grey Ghost and Bishop's Blessing. Trout are all rainbows, again averaging 0.9–1.4 kg (2–3 lb).

Lake Rotomahana is possibly the least fished of any of the Rotorua lakes because of its access, which is limited to a fine-weather road at the end of Ashpit Road which passes Lake Rerewhakaaitu. This means that anglers need to have a boat, preferably a light one on a light trailer. Because the lake is a bird sanctuary, no motors on boats are permitted during May. This lake produces excellent rainbows running from 1.8–2.7 kg (4–6 lb), which are said to be among the purest in the district. Fishing is best late in the season, March to June. Trolling is best using medium sinking fly line and streamer fly. Spinning is also popular on this lake, with Zed Spinner being most favoured. However, by far the most trout are taken by fly fishing using slow-sinking line—same flies as for Lake Rerewhakaaitu.

Lakes Okareka and Tikitapu (Blue Lake). Both lakes hold only rainbows and have limited road access, so best fishing is to be had by using boats.

Lake Okareka is predominantly a trolling lake and trolling is best using medium sinking fly line and streamer fly at the eastern end of the lake, close inshore. The best fly fishing is to be had at the outlet of the lake in May and June, with similar flies as for other Rotorua lakes. The best fish taken from this lake for a number of years was caught at Easter 1977 by a 16-year-old boy, Kevin Stevens; it weighed 4.2 kg (9½ lb) and was taken trolling. This was an exceptional fish for this lake, which normally produces an average weight of 0.9–1.5 kg (2–3½ lb).

Lake Tikitapu has no spawning streams so is referred to as a trolling lake. There is fly fishing available along the beach near the road late in the season, but swimmers and water-skiers interfere with any concentrated fly fishing from the beach. Trolling with sinking fly lines is best, using green Toby or Flamingo or the dark streamers such as Kilwell and Mrs Simpson. Rainbows here are averaging up to 1.4 kg (3 lb) and fish up to 3.2 kg (7 lb) have been taken in recent seasons. Brook trout (*fontinalis*) were liberated in the Blue Lake in 1978.

Green Lake (Rotokakahi). This lake is not dealt with as it is closed to all anglers except the owners.

LAKE TAUPO

This lake has been described as the greatest trout factory in the world and certainly lives up to that reputation. One is always hearing

stories that the fishing is not as good as it used to be, but in twenty years of fishing on Taupo I have never found it any different. It is still as good as the first time I ever went there, with two qualifications. The trout are better now than they were twenty years ago; then they averaged 0.9 kg (2 lb), now they average 1.4–2.0 kg (3–4½ lb). Again, there seem to be just as many fish there, though today there are three times as many anglers to share the fabulous bonanza—which, I guess, is how it should be.

There are both rainbow and brown trout in the lake, but rainbows are more prevalent. In the past ten years or so the average ranged from 1.4–2.0 kg (3–4½ lb) but 2.3–2.7 kg (5–6 lb) trout are caught weekly and each year sees extra large rainbows of 4.5 kg (10 lb) and

Three anglers admire the evening serenity of the Duchess pool, Tongariro River

131

Three anchored boats with anglers fishing the Tongariro delta or, more correctly, one of the four mouths where the river enters Lake Taupo (see page 135). Note the rip visible by the left-hand boat

over taken. The browns run heavier, averaging 2.3 kg (5 lb), with the heaviest taken in recent years weighing 8.2 kg (18 lb).

Like Lake Rotorua, Taupo is open to fishing all year round. The two favoured methods of fishing its waters are streamer fly on sinking line, either fly fishing or trolling. There is little or no spinning done, but of recent years nymph fishing on the spawning streams has become increasingly popular.

This lake trolls exceptionally well all year round but there are two main periods in the year when conditions and methods differ. Over the spring months, from October to Christmas, the trolling is at its best using normal fly lines with streamer flies such as Parsons' Glory, Grey Ghost or Taupo Tiger. When using these streamer flies a long leader is recommended, up to 9 metres (30 ft) and of lighter breaking strain than the usual 4 kg. As a rule this type of trolling is done parallel to shore and is good anywhere around the lake on both the eastern and western shores as well as the famous Horomatangi Reef. Incidentally, a good procedure for judging the right distance from shore without the aid of a depth-finder, is to position yourself where you can see the bottom of the lake over one side of the boat but not from the other side. This will place you right on the lip of deeper water and if you follow this contour with your fly as near to the bottom as you can manage you will be in productive water.

From Christmas through autumn and on through the winter trout seek deeper climes, so trollers need to go on lead lines and themselves move out to deeper water. Lead lines fish equally well either with a streamer fly (such as Parsons' Glory) or with spoons or spinners. The Taupo trollers' favourite for the past few seasons has been the green Cobra in small size; and second in popularity would be the black or the green Toby, with Mother of Pearl occasionally producing well.

Turning to fly fishing, it is the stream-mouth fishing on Lake Taupo which has made the lake world famous, combined of course with the popularity of the upstream fishing in rivers like the Tongariro and Tauranga-Taupo. Clockwise from Taupo township the main spawning streams and rivers entering the lake are: Waitahanui, Hinemaiaia, Tauranga-Taupo, Waimarino, Waiotaka, Tongariro, Kuratau, Whareroa, Whanganui, Waihaha, Waihora. Of these the Tongariro is important enough to be dealt with in a separate section to follow.

Standing in waders at the mouths of all these streams and casting a fast-sinking fly line with streamer fly will produce good fishing from October to February, and especially good when the smelt are running within that period. The fishing is mainly at its best morning or evening on into dark, but is good even during the day when smelt are running. Smelt will not be so evident from March until June, but the mouths fish well during this period as spawning runs are gathering momentum.

Christmas and almost the whole of January should be avoided by serious anglers because of holidaymakers, campers, swimmers and water-skiers doing everything but considering a fisherman's peace of mind.

The eastern side of Taupo has good road access, as the main highway crosses all the streams flowing into the lake, most of which have side roads running up them for a short distance. The streams themselves fish well with streamer fly October to Christmas, and are at their best in May and June when trout are running up them to spawn. It is in these latter months that nymphing is very productive.

Western Bay, having no road access, is a favourite haunt of mine as either boat or float plane is needed to get there. The area is becoming increasingly popular, for now it is rare to have a river mouth to oneself whereas a few years back this was no problem. However, a boat makes it possible to move from rip to rip and, perhaps even these

133

days, find one for yourself. It will pay, incidentally, to carry a shovel so that a seldom-fished rip can be straightened out and made fishable until the next easterly again turns it side-on to the shore.

During the summer smelting one can cast a fly from any beach around this lake away from stream mouths with equal success. At this time, too, a spinner rod can be used—in fact, during smelting is the only time I have ever seen one used. Most popular streamer flies are Parsons' Glory with yellow and green body, Taupo Tiger, Grey Ghost, Mrs Simpson, Hamill's Killer and Kilwell. At night, Black Phantom, Hairy Dog, Ewe Wasp, Taihape Tickler, Craig's Night.

Spinners as above—Cobra, Toby in black or green, Flatfish, Mother of Pearl, Zed Spinner and Hot Shot.

The largest trout ever weighed and recorded from this lake was a 27½ lb (12.4 kg) rainbow female taken in 1924 on a fly at the north of the Waitahanui River. It was mounted and displayed in the Taupo Lake Hotel but was destroyed by fire in 1951. Recommended reading for these waters is *Taupo Fishing Diary* by Alex Gillett.

TONGARIRO RIVER AND DELTA

This is the biggest river flowing into Lake Taupo, the main spawning river, and the most famous of all North Island rivers. It has white-water rapids, deep pools and long reaches spreading out until they too dissolve into turbulent rapids. It is a river just made for shooting-head lines and streamer flies. The trout are predominantly rainbows in the middle and upper reaches, although large browns favour the lower sluggish portions.

·As it is a spawning river, there are few fish remaining in it during the summer, so the best fishing is from September to Christmas, when the trout are dropping down to the lake, or again from April onwards, when the autumn runs are starting. During summer the few remaining fish can be taken successfully with nymphs.

I prefer the 'April onwards' period, for then the fish are in excellent condition and are averaging 2.7–3.6 kg (6–8 lb). The best period is nevertheless considered May onwards—after the school holidays and on weekdays rather than weekends, when it will be less crowded.

The runs can often move through very quickly and at other times take days, so it is a river that needs a 'grapevine' of information, very much like when the salmon are running in the South Island. This river is fished very much the same as fishing steelhead rivers in the American north-west so is very popular with visiting Americans (see page 163). The river when crowded requires anglers' etiquette in that you should never sit on a pool but move down after each cast to let others follow. This practice should really apply everywhere in New

Zealand. Popular flies are the Red Setter, Maribou, Hamill's and similar nymphs. All pools are well signposted from the main highway and good walking tracks give access to both banks. Recommended reading about the river is *Trout of the Tongariro* by Tony Jensen, and Gary Kemsley's *Taupo Fishing Guide*.

At the delta where it enters the lake the river splits into four streams or mouths known as Blind Mouth, First Mouth, the Hook and Main Mouth. The best access to these is by boat from the new launching ramps and marina situated at the end of the tail-race at Tokaanu. Depending on the speed of the boat, it takes only five to ten minutes to reach the delta. The four mouths run across a shallow bar seldom more than 0.4 metres deep (18 in) and then drop off into approximately 18 metres (60 ft) of water. It is therefore a dangerous place to wade in chest waders, because the lip can give way easily and put you feet up in a matter of seconds. By far the safest and best method is to anchor the boat in shallow water so that the stern is over the drop off, and cast from the boat.

High-density, weight-forward line is recommended, preferably a number 10 to get your fly down. A long line should be cast out, and

Headwaters of the finest dry-fly river in the North Island if not the world—the Rangitikei. Here Jock Graham, fishing guide of Taupo, holds a splendid deep-water rainbow weighing 5.8 kg (13 lb). Best access to this remote location is by helicopter

135

you should wait long enough to allow the line to sink to the bottom before starting to retrieve. The fly on the retrieve should follow the bottom contour up, so that fish can strike anywhere from the bottom to the lip. There are usually other boats fishing this popular spot and one simply anchors alongside them. However, if you can get there first, it does pay to move the boat until your line when cast out drops straight down, not out to either side. If it goes straight down then you are right in the centre of the rip and in a good fish-catching position.

The delta fishes surprisingly well all summer from November to March, although February and March are the favoured times. Even April, depending on the season, can produce excellent results. Best flies are Red Setter, yellow Parsons', Hamill's, Kilwell, Taupo Tiger and the recently designed lure-flies called Glo-bugs and Nobblers, they get results.

In March of 1976 I received an urgent request to send eight large rainbows packed in ice to a diplomatic dinner. The only time I could get away was after work and the day—a weekday—happened to be the full moon. The delta is possibly the best stream mouth at such a time as the fly goes deep down.

I left home after work to drive the 144 km to the delta and on the way called in to ask Bob Sullivan, the fly-fishing guide and tackle dealer at Taupo, to join me. Bob was willing and able, but it wasn't until well after dark that we arrived at the launching ramp, though the full moon allowed us to find the Hook easily enough. I anchored the boat, moved it twice to get into the right position, then Bob and I started to fish.

We had the whole place to ourselves and couldn't have picked a more beautiful and calm night. It would have been after eight o'clock when we started but within minutes we were both tied into fish, having both used Black Phantom streamer flies. By eleven o'clock we had the eight required rainbows aboard the boat. The smallest weighed 1.5 kg (3½ lb) and the biggest 3.4 kg (7½ lb). Besides our catch, we had lost a fish or two each, and altogether we had been almost continuously playing trout during those three hours. I also hooked several kouras, which showed that my line was where it should have been—right on the bottom.

Fishing of that rewarding kind is certainly not untypical of the Tongariro delta area. Joe King of Spokane took a 4.5 kg rainbow (10 lb) during the day at the same spot in April 1977 and I guided Ed Zern of *Field and Stream* magazine, who took two seven-pounders there that same year on consecutive casts.

In November 1982, Margarette Coutts and Tony Hayes opened a welcome addition to the fishing amenities in the area, the Tongariro

Fishing Lodge, which has become extremely popular with visiting local, and overseas anglers. One of their many distinguished guests, ex-president Jimmy Carter of the US, landed an excellent conditioned 3.62 kg (8 lb) rainbow hen at the delta in February 1984. In September of the same year, another guest landed a beautiful 4.64 kg (10.25 lb) rainbow out of the river near the lodge. These big fish just keep on getting caught. Because of the excellent fishing and the publicity given to the region, the Tongariro has become a most sought-after fishing destination. This often causes some angler congestion on the favourite pools, especially at the weekends. Even so, the quality of the fish, and the numbers available, have not diminished. I suggest you try to plan your fishing for mid-week and off-season times. Recommended reading is the excellent monthly colour magazine published at Turangi called *Fly Fisher*.

LAKES ROTOAIRA AND OTAMANGAKAU

Both these lakes are reached from the Tokaanu-Chateau road which runs between them, Rotoaira lying to the south and Otamangakau, a newly-formed hydro lake, to the north of the road.

Rotoaira has long been famous as an easy lake in which to catch lots of fish. In fact, before the changes brought about by hydro development guides could virtually take clients there on a no fish-no pay basis, success guaranteed. Since then the lake level has been raised, among other things, and the fish are now harder to come by. However, as the main spawning stream remains unchanged and the lake is stocked annually, the fishing by present-day standards is still good. As well as a Taupo licence, anglers must procure an entry permit from the Rotoaira Trust Board. Its headquarters are on the lake and this is where U-drive and guide boats are available.

It is a lake which caters for trollers, spinners and wet-fly angling at the canal outlets. It was at two of these hydro outlets, incidentally, that we caught the rainbows for the William Conrad ('Cannon' of TV fame) American Broadcasting Company's film made in 1975. These rainbows were readily taken during the daytime on Mrs Simpson streamer flies. On the same occasion two of us fishing in the one boat with a cameraman caught sixteen rainbows one day just to film 'jump shots'—trout jumping above water.

Lake Rotoaira fishes well all through the open season. The main method by day is trolling, either with a streamer fly or spinners. Spin fishing from a drifting or anchored boat is popular. Rainbows average 0.9–1.4 kg (2–3 lb) but I myself have taken a 2.7 kg rainbow (6 lb) and in 1974 saw a ten-pounder caught (4.5 kg). The best spinners to use are

Toby, Penny and Cobra; the best streamer flies, Mrs Simpson, Black Phantom, Turkey green, Hamill's green and Kilwell.

Otamangakau, as stated, is a hydro lake with its outlet canal flowing into Lake Rotoaira. Like all newly-formed lakes, it will fish well for the first few years until it settles down. Trout grow quickly with the abundance of food available. It is a very shallow lake with a heavy weed growth, and is fished mainly with fly and spinner from the shore by anglers wearing waders. It trolls quite well if one can stick to the deep canals, but most troll with fly lines because of the shallow water. Trout were taken in 1977 up to 2.7 kg (6 lb). Flies and spinners as for Lake Rotoaira. As recently as 1978–9 I had excellent fishing on this lake, using a sink-tip floating line from shore with a size-14 nymph. Nymphing is now the most favoured method on this lake, for in 1983, five 4.53 kg (10 lb) rainbows were taken by the one angler in the one week by this method.

NORTHLAND

The waters of Northland have generally been considered too warm for trout to survive, and therefore few anglers travel there to fish them. Enthusiastic local societies have nevertheless made regular liberations over the years and as a result have made some very good angling for themselves.

The principal waters are the Kai Iwi Lakes north of Dargaville, the Kaihu River and the Wairoa River system, especially in the Hikurangi-Whakapara region. The streams are predominantly dry fly, and produce rainbow trout of 0.5–0.9 kg (1–2 lb) average. The Kai Iwi Lakes, in a sandy coastal area reached by gravel road, produce some very good fishing for trout to 1.0 kg and in 1975 several rainbows were taken there from 2.7–3.6 kg (6–8 lb) which would have given Taupo trout a run for their money. These are mainly taken on streamer flies such as Hamill's Killer, Mrs Simpson or Kilwell. The best time to fish the district is either early or late in the season.

SOUTH AUCKLAND

South of Auckland the principal fishing areas are the Waikato River and its tributaries, notably the extensive Waipa River system plus the Waihou (Thames) River and tributaries. These three main areas are often neglected by visiting and local anglers in their rush to get to the popular locations of Rotorua and Taupo. This, I feel, is a mistake, for the region offers some of the best dry-fly fishing in the North Island. As well, it provides plenty of variety, such as spinning and trolling on the hydro lakes between Taupo and Karapiro. In their lower reaches the three rivers are slow, deep and sluggish, which gives excellent

(Opposite) Lower pool of the Hoporuahine Falls in the gorge of the same name west of Lake Waikaremoana. From the falls down is one of the finest stretches of fly water flowing to this lake

139

spinning water for large trout up to 4.5 kg (10 lb). However, it is the upper reaches which not only provide the spawning grounds but the excellent dry-fly fishing that has so far received little attention.

WAIHOU WATERSHED

With Okoroire as headquarters, you would be within a few miles of the Oraka, Waimakariri, Waimou, Kakahu and Omahine streams. These all rise in the Kaimai Range, are fine gravel-bottomed streams flowing through native bush in the upper reaches and grassy farmlands in the lower before joining the Waihou. They provide very good dry-fly fishing for rainbows averaging 0.5–0.9 kg (1–2 lb) during morning and evening rises, with wet-fly fishing during the heat of the day.

WAIKATO STREAMS

Putaruru makes an ideal location to fish the Waihou streams as above, and additionally the Pokaiwhenua and Little Waipa streams crossed by the Putaruru-Arapuni road. These, similar to the Waihou streams, are fished the same and produce similar sized trout. They also provide good wet-fly fishing where they join the Waikato River, where trout over 1.8 kg (4 lb) are taken annually.

WAIPA WATERSHED

Otorohanga, situated on the Waipa River, makes a good head-quarters within an easy drive of the Mangatutu, Mangaokewa, Moakurarua, Puniu and Ngutunui streams. They rise mostly in native bush areas and flow though lush farmlands in the lower reaches and provide both rainbow and brown trout averaging 0.5–0.9 kg (1–2 lb), although fish up to 2.3 kg (5 lb) are taken from seldom-fished pools. These streams are fished the same as those in the previous two areas, with dry fly being the most popular, although spinning is allowed on some waters.

Favoured flies for all three localities are Lacewing, Black Sedge, March Brown, Twilight Beauty, Red-tipped Governor and nymphs. Wet flies favoured are Claret and Mallard, Kakahi Queen, Royal Coachman and Twilight Beauty. Streamers such as Mrs Simpson and Hamill's are popular where streams join the Waikato River.

HYDRO LAKES OF THE WAIKATO

Dams built on the Waikato River have created lakes, in ascending order, at Karapiro, Arapuni, Waipapa, Maraetai, Whakamaru,

Atiamuri and Ohakuri; those above Maraetai dam are open all year round. They all provide trolling, wet-fly fishing, spinning and good evening rises for dry fly.

Rainbows predominate, though browns are found in all seven lakes. Trout average 0.9–1.4 kg (2–3 lb) in this system, but much heavier weights are caught regularly, especially below the power station outlets where a plentiful food supply is chopped up for them in the turbines. Where side streams enter the lakes are favoured spots for fly and spin fishing, and the lakes are recommended as some of the best spinning water available in the North Island.

Of recent years, with the enriching of these lakes mainly through aerial topdressing runoff, the weed growth has been prolific in most of them, causing problems for trollers. I am constantly amazed that they receive so little attention from anglers, as they are grossly underfished, with most vacationing anglers bypassing them in favour of the more popular lakes of Rotorua and Taupo. Limit bags from trollers and spin fishermen are common, and in 1976 two rainbows of 5.4 kg (12 lb) were taken on streamer flies in the gorge below the Arapuni power station.

Popular flies are: Streamers—Mrs Simpson, Kilwell, Hamill's green, Scotch Poacher, Red Setter. Wets—Claret and Mallard, Royal Coachman, Twilight Beauty. Dries—Lacewing, Stonefly, Hardy's Favourite, and nymphs. Spinners—Cobra, Toby, Flatfish, Mother of Pearl, Billy Hill and Minnow.

TARANAKI WATERSHEDS

The streams in this area rise in the snowfields of Mount Egmont and from that central source flow to the Tasman Sea almost in a complete circle. Anglers have excellent access, as all streams are crossed by roads or have roads running parallel to them for most of their fishable distance. The predominant species is the brown, but rainbows are found in most of them with average weights of from 0.5–0.9 kg (1–2 lb). Fish of 1.4–1.8 kg (3–4 lb) are caught annually.

The principal river north of the mountain is the Waitara, more especially its chief tributary, the Manganui, the largest carrying trout and considered one of the best, where browns have been averaging 1.4 kg. Best feeder streams of the Manganui are the Maketawa and Ngatoro, which can be reached from the Inglewood-Midhurst road.

From Waitara, travelling south to Hawera around the coast, the following main trout streams are crossed: Waiongana, Waiwakaiho, Mangorei, Te Henui, Tapuae, Oakura, Timaru, Kaihihi, Stony, Waiweranui, Warea, Kopoaiaia, Okahu, Oanui, Waiaua, Mangahume, Taungatara, Kaupokonui, Kapuni, Waingongoro. The Kaupokonui River, with numerous tributaries, is the largest south of the mountain. It is very productive and yields trout averaging 0.9–1.4 kg (2–3 lb), with annual top weights of 1.8–2.7 kg (4–6 lb).

In all Taranaki streams creeper, grasshopper and minnows are good fish catchers early in the season, but in the summer months fly fishing comes into its own. Suggested flies are Black Gnat, Peveril's Peak, Greenwell's Glory, Red-tipped Governor and Hardy's Favourite. Nymph fishing is most popular.

WANGANUI WATERSHED

The Wanganui is one of the largest rivers in the North Island and from Taumarunui down is open for natural and artificial bait fishing, making it, like the Waikato, another outstanding spinning river. The predominant species is the brown but rainbows are also found in it, with some of the tributaries offering mainly rainbows. The average trout runs to 1.4 kg (3 lb) but fish in the 2.3–2.7 kg range (5–6 lb) are not uncommon.

The headwaters of the river and the tributaries Whakapapa and Mangatepopo have suffered not only from hydro diversions but from an almost annual volcanic eruption by Mount Ruapehu with consequent mineral pollution. Thus the fishing above Manunui can be unreliable. However, other main tributaries are unaffected by this mineralisation and their cleansing action on the main river gives it a remarkable recovery rate after each eruption. North of Taumarunui are the Waimiha and Ongarue, both excellent dry-fly streams and the best now of the northern tributaries, where the trout are averaging 0.9 kg (2 lb).

RANGITIKEI RIVER

I consider this to be one of the best trout-fishing rivers in New Zealand, producing some of the biggest trout in the country, especially in its upper reaches where it has been neglected by anglers. It is a long river, flowing south for nearly 250 kilometres from its source east of the Kaimanawa Mountains. Near Utiku, about half its length from the sea, it is joined by two major tributaries, the Hautapu and the Moawhango. The Hautapu is very highly regarded as a dry-fly stream, yielding fish up to 1.8 kg (4 lb) and I know of one weighing 4.5 kg (10 lb) taken two seasons ago on a dry. The Moawhango also rises in the rugged country of the Kaimanawas and its Waiouru watershed, incidentally, has one of the largest populations of brook trout (*fontinalis*) in the North Island.

Jim Rizzuto, fishing writer from Hawaii, holds up a 1.8 kg (4 lb) rainbow taken from Lake Taupo on a harling rig

In its lower reaches the Rangitikei fishes best between Bulls and Utiku, a long stretch where the river has a bed of 'papa' (mudstone) and shingle and which is accessible from the main north-south highway and side roads. Trout here have been averaging 0.9–1.4 kg (2–3 lb) and are taken mainly on minnow lures, although dry and wet flies will take fish at the mouths of side streams rising in the Ruahine Ranges to the east. Suggested lures: Colorado Spinner, Mepps, Devon, Minnow. Streamer flies: Mrs Simpson, Hamill's, Kilwell, Red Setter. Dries: Stonefly nymphs, Mayfly, Hardy's Favourite, Blue Dunn, March Brown.

The upper reaches north of the Taihape-Napier road are really at

143

the back of beyond, with access only by walking, on horseback or by helicopter from Taupo. There are endless stretches of primitive water which is crystal clear, not unlike that of the Worsley or the Clinton in Fiordland, and some of the pools are all of ten metres deep. However, stories of the fabulous fishing have increased the angling pressure on this river to the extent that it is in danger of becoming over-fished. I would strongly recommend that anglers visiting this 'experience of a lifetime' river, practise 'catch and release'. Too many anglers have flown out their entire catch, and have paid little regard to preserving this fishery for future generations. In this locality the trout are predominantly rainbows, with the average running as high as 2.3 kg (5 lb) and several recent catches made of the order of 3.6–4.1 kg (8–9 lb). I also know of a 6.3 kg fish (14 lb) caught there not long ago, and I have seen trout in some of the pools which I conservatively estimate could weigh 9.0 kg (20 lb).

I have visited these remote upper regions of the river many times, using all three means of transport but of late mostly by helicopter. The first few visits were with hunters who happened to have spin rods along, and although the fish were impressive, the fishing by this method on such a great river was not. Of recent years I have taken several fly fishermen to the river and, by comparison, fishing by this method is a revelation. Indeed, I would like to see this water classified as 'fly only' to preserve it for all time.

Dry-fly fishing, however, is not without its difficulties if one approaches the large pools from below. During daylight most trout are lying at the tail end of the pools and in the clear water they invariably spook and dart away to stay deep in the deep blue water. Geoff Thomas, the Rotorua guide, encountered this problem with the famous golfer Jack Nicklaus, for they fished with only a dry fly and failed to make a catch.

From this and other experiences I worked out that to take the large trout in these pools—and some of them are monsters—one would have to fish from the top of the pool and try to get a nymph or sinking fly down to the fish lying at the tail end. In March 1978 I flew into the river by helicopter with the well known American angler Ernie Schweibert, author of *Matching the Hatch* and *Nymphs*, and Kerney Towers and Charlie Carniglia of Santa Rosa, California. I recommended to these anglers that they fished downstream and used nymphs, preferably weighted, and a fast-sinking line. This method worked exceptionally well, far exceeding expectations. Kerney and Charlie both ran out of nymphs after a time but I then found that a size-8 Red Setter, Mrs Simpson, Kilwell and the like worked equally well. We caught more fish than we needed and returned ninety per cent alive to the water. The biggest for the day weighed 4.65 kg (10¼ lb) and the smallest 2.0 kg (4½ lb).

MANAWATU RIVER SYSTEM

The Manawatu River rises on the eastern side of the Ruahine Range and flows through a gorge to the western side and then to the Tasman Sea. The main river produces average-weight brown trout of about 0.9 kg (2 lb) but fish to 2.7 kg (6 lb) in the lower reaches. The best fishing is from Shannon upstream through the gorge, where it is preferred spinning water. The principal trout-holding tributary streams are the Pohangina, joining it on the western side of the range, and the Mangatainoka, joining it on the eastern side. The latter is considered the best fly-fishing river, producing trout averaging 1.4 kg (3 lb) over its 43-km length. The Makakaki, Tiraumea and Makuri, all farther west of the Mangatainoka, are good dry-fly streams producing mainly smaller trout than the parent river. All four have good access from Pahiatua.

The main river produces well on Minnow, Devon, Wedge and Mepps. Flies favoured on the tributaries are mayfly and stone nymphs, Red-tipped Governor, Hardy's Favourite, Blue Dunn and March Brown.

RUAMAHANGA RIVER SYSTEM

This river and lake system provides the best fishing in the Wairarapa and is very handy to Wellington, with the towns of Masterton and Featherston more central to the fishing. The river rises on the north-eastern slopes of the Tararua Range and has four main tributaries, the Waipoua, Waingawa, Mangatere and Waiohine streams. As well, the Tauherenikau joins the system at Lake Wairarapa, and the Tauweru River joins the main river from the east at Gladstone. The main river is around 128 km in length and has produced very good brown trout averaging 0.9–1.4 kg (2–3 lb) over the past few seasons. The tributaries produce slightly smaller averages, with the Waipoua being the recommended dry-fly stream. Lake Wairarapa has a large population of perch as well as brown trout.

Suggested flies same as for the Manawatu.

HAWKE'S BAY WATERS

With its variety of fishing water, this area rivals Rotorua and Taupo, for not only does it have five large river systems but lakes Waikaremoana and Waikare Iti as well. Both rainbow and brown

(Overleaf) *The picturesque Maharakeke Stream, tributary of the Tukituki River, is one of the top dry-fly streams of Hawke's Bay*

trout averaging 0.9–1.8kg (2–4lb) are found in most systems, hinterland rivers regularly produce fish weighing 2.7–4.0kg (6–9lb) and trout up to 9kg (20lb) have been caught with surprising regularity at the power station outlets on the Waikare-Taheke River.

Starting in the south, the rivers are the Maraetotara, a meadow-bank stream providing fly-only fishing for browns averaging 0.5–0.9kg (1–2lb); it fishes well on a dry. Next is the large Tukituki River with the Maharakeke, Makaretu, Tukipo, Waipawa and Mangaonuku as its tributaries. Access is good to all these streams from Waipawa and Waipukurau. Fishing is mainly with spinners on the main river, using Minnow, Devon, Wedge or Mepps. Some of the tributaries are fly only, producing very good nymph, dry or wet fly fishing for both rainbows and browns.

The Ngaruroro River rises in the Kaimanawa Mountains and flows to the sea near Napier. It provides both rainbow and brown fishing, although spinning is the most favoured method. Access to the lower regions is good from the Napier-Taihape road and it is now possible to fly into the headwaters to the Boyd strip from Taupo. In these headwaters nymphing with a six-metre leader is recommended because the fish are line-shy in the clear water. They average 1.4 to 1.8 kg (3-4 lb) but have been taken up to 3.2 kg (7 lb) and one taken in 1977 tipped the scales at 5.4 kg (12 lb). However, like the Rangitikei River, demand for a fly-in remote experience is placing increased angling pressure on this fine piece of water.

Third of the big rivers is the Tutaekuri, having the Mangaone as its main tributary. The latter fishes best in its lower reaches, and the main river best downstream from the Mangaone junction. Both fish equally well with fly or spinner.

The Mohaka is one of the best rivers rising on the northern slopes of the Kaimanawas, having the Oamaru, Ripia, Waipunga, Te Hoe and Hautapu as tributaries. It carries rainbows and browns averaging 0.9–1.4kg (2–3lb), but I have caught fish in it up to 3.2kg (7lb). Access to headwaters is achieved by flying to the Oamaru strip from Taupo, while the middle reaches and the Waipunga are fished from the Napier-Taupo road. Some of the best Mohaka fishing is to be had near its junction with the Te Hoe, also in the Te Hoe and Hautapu tributaries where fish to 3.2kg (7lb) are not uncommon. Spinners and wet and dry flies can all be used with equal success.

To fish almost the entire length of the Mohaka it is now possible to charter a guide from Taupo with inflatable rubber rafts, which he flies along with camping gear to the headwaters airstrip on Oamaru Stream. The party then float down the 60-km stretch to the main highway bridge on the Napier-Taupo road, or carry on a further

30 km to the road end at the junction with the Hautapu.

Possibly the most widespread river system in Hawke's Bay is that of the Wairoa River, which has the Waiau, Waikare-Taheke, Ruakituri and Hangaroa rivers as its main tributaries. Like the Rangitikei, this is one of the top river systems in the country and provides some fabulous fishing. Road access from Wairoa is good for the entire length of the Waikare-Taheke and most of the Hangaroa, and to the lower reaches of the Waiau and Ruakituri. Wet fly, dry fly and spinning are equally successful. Access to the headwaters of the Waiau is difficult and mainly gained by walking in from Ruatahuna, but the fishing is well worth while, for catches average 1.4 kg (3 lb) and often reach 2.3–3.2 kg (5–7 lb). Likewise, access above the waterfall in the Ruakituri is by walking, but it is especially good around the Anini junction, where I have seen fish taken from 2.3–4.5 kg (5–10 lb). The middle reaches of the Ruakituri, in my opinion is one of the finest dry-fly fishing stretches in the North Island, for both brown and rainbows. In the mid-fifties, I had some of my best fishing experiences learning to cast on this river, while working as a ranger based at Ruatahuna.

Suggested spinners are Cobra, Toby, Mepps, Minnow, Zed Spinner and Wedge. Smelt-pattern flies are recommended, and dries such as the Red-tipped Governor, Coachman, Black Gnat, Green Beetle, Lacewing and Stonefly.

LAKE WAIKAREMOANA

Waikaremoana is a beautiful bush-surrounded lake in the heart of Urewera National Park, reached from the Rotorua-Wairoa road. It has both rainbows and browns averaging 0.9–1.4 kg (2–3 lb) but often running to 1.8–2.3 kg (4–5 lb). The lake trolls well and provides good wet-fly fishing at the stream mouths, which fish well early and late in the season. The feeder streams, Hoporuahine, Mokau and Aniwaniwa, are accessible from the highway, but other streams such as the Wairau are only accessible by boat. This is a good lake in which to spot cruising fish from rocky outcrops and cast for them, and spinning is popular for this reason.

The streams accessible by road provide very good wet-fly fishing in May and June and especially when the lake level has been low enough for the streams entering the lake to have a well defined rip. I have repeatedly taken limit bags by casting a fast-sinking line and streamer fly, exactly the same as fished at Rotorua or Taupo, so it is a most productive lake. I have always found that the Hoporuahine River, in the stretch between the waterfall and the lake, fishes as well in May and June as the Tongariro. It is a short stretch of water, but when the spawning runs have started it provides excellent fishing with shooting-head line and Red Setter fly.

My experience of spinning on this lake has also been very good using a small brass Wedge; it outfished anything else in my tackle box. Suggested flies are Red Setter, Parsons' Glory and Hamill's. Spinners are the Wedge, Cobra, Toby, Flatfish and Billy Hill. Popular dries are Lacewing, Stonefly, March Brown and nymphs.

LAKE WAIKARE ITI

This small lake is situated to the north of Lake Waikaremoana and is reached by a climbing walk of half an hour to an hour from Aniwaniwa, depending on how fit you are. Where Waikaremoana has both rainbow and brown trout, Waikare Iti has rainbows only, which average about 0.9 kg (2 lb). The lake fishes exceptionally well in and around December when the larger lake is most difficult. There are walking tracks right round it for access, and in the summer there are boats for hire. Streamer flies such as Kilwell, Mrs Simpson, Parsons' Glory and Red Setter are used. Latterly I have heard of anglers who have had excellent results nymphing.

BAY OF PLENTY RIVERS

Of the seven main rivers entering the Bay of Plenty, five rise in the Urewera Country—the Motu, Waioeka, Waiotahi, Whakatane and Rangitaiki. The other two, the Tarawera and Kaituna rivers, are outlets of Lakes Tarawera, Rotorua and Rotoiti.

The best fishing river is the Rangitaiki. With its tributaries, the Horomanga, Whirinaki and Wheao, it provides some of the finest dry-fly fishing in the region, easiest access being from Murupara. Trout, both rainbow and brown, are averaging up to 0.9 kg (2 lb), but every year one sees fish taken in the range 2.3–2.7 kg (5–6 lb).

The Wheao River, once one of the finest dry-fly rivers in the country, has been lost forever it seems, due to the erection of a dam, and the subsequent flood and washout when part of the dam-canal collapsed. The engineers at the 'water right' application hearing, before the dam was started, were warned of this possibility, but angler advice was ignored. Anglers beware, it can happen again on other rivers, so we must make ourselves heard if the same ignorance is to be prevented in the future. With the demise of the Wheao, the stretch of the Rangitaiki which flows through the Kaingaroa forest, has now come into prominence as a fine stretch of dry-fly water. It is a delightful stretch of river, but permits to enter the forest must be obtained from the NZ Forest Service at either Rotorua or Murupara.

Another alternative, is the new hydro-lake Aniwhenua, situated further down the Rangitaiki at Galatea. This lake fishes best from a boat, and is producing excellent fish with a nymph, or sink-tip line and such as a Kilwell streamer fly.

The Whirinaki is also a favourite dry-fly river and fishes exceptionally well late in the season with nymphs. Unlike South Island rivers, pools here are closer together, which means a fabulous amount of fishing for little walking distance or ground covered, a winning feature of most of these Urewera streams.

The Whakatane River has the Waimana as its main tributary, the latter being the most favoured dry-fly water in this system; its lower reaches are fished from Whakatane. The headwaters of the Whakatane, reached from Ruatahuna, provide very good dry-fly water, although spinners are the most favoured. Trout here have been averaging around 0.9 kg (2 lb), with 1.8-kg fish (4 lb) not uncommon. Much of the Waioeka River runs parallel to the Opotiki to Gisborne inland road, which also crosses the upper Motu; both rivers provide good dry-fly water, with nymphing proving very successful. The lower reaches of the Motu are not as good as the headwaters.

In all the above Urewera rivers and streams I have found that during the day, when hatches are scarce, dry fly will produce mainly small trout unless casting for a specific trout. Switching to a sinking-tip line with nymphs can have surprising results.

The Tarawera and Kaituna rivers produce good fishing downstream from their falls. The fish are predominantly rainbows and average 0.9–1.4 kg (2–3 lb), though 2.7-kg fish (6 lb) are taken regularly. Dry fly is most productive in the upper reaches and spinning favoured lower down.

The water from the trout pool down to the enclosing bush on the Kaituna, although limited, is one of the finest pieces of dry-fly water handy to the city of Rotorua. It is also a peaceful beauty spot and a photographer's dream. It produces one of the best evening rises anywhere in New Zealand, rivalled only by the 'mad rise' on the Mataura in Southland. Two casting jetties have been erected by the local angling club at chosen spots and the rest of the banks have easy access. Purists despair, this stretch of water has now been opened to spin fishermen.

Suggested flies for all the rivers are Lacewing, Green Beetle, Black Gnat, Red-tipped Governor, March Brown and nymphs.

NOTE: Access to most rivers and streams is across private property, so before fishing the owner should be approached for permission. This is seldom refused. Indeed, in many cases the farmer will advise on the best pools and methods.

South Island Trout Fishing Locations

In the South Island the Southern Lakes and Mataura River areas have, like Taupo and Rotorua in the North, received most publicity and therefore most attention from visiting anglers. The high-quality fishing these two areas offer has made them popular for guided trips and the availability of guides has in turn tended to concentrate more tourist activity upon them. But where I pointed out for the North Island that there is an enormous amount of largely untried fishing water to be explored outside the popular centres, the same applies to the South Island. The fame of Southern Lakes-Mataura should be weighed against dozens of other productive waterways throughout the island. The Waitaki watershed, for instance, is fast becoming the new 'accepted' place to fish, and the vast Westland fishery, with improved access in the form of plane and helicopter landing strips used by venison hunters and whitebaiters, now presents unbelievable fishing opportunities.

In the course of my work I have in recent years received more requests to fish the South Island than the North Island, even counting Taupo. One attraction the south has is the obvious one that far fewer anglers are found there—the desire that lots of fishermen have to get away from overcrowded places. Another main factor, however, is that dry-fly fishing is now the most popular method practised by world-travelling anglers. For that reason alone the South Island stands out as one of the world's best trout-fishing destinations.

As with the North Island, I cannot hope to cover every stream, river and lake but the main locations described will provide starting-points for further forays into the various districts. Since it is the South Island, I will deal first with the two most favoured areas, Southern Lakes and Southland, move on to Otago and the Waitaki, then 'go west' and travel round the top of the island to the east.

Salmon fishing as distinct from trout fishing is a special feature of the South Island angling scene. Salmon types and main locations are discussed in detail at the end of this chapter (page 175), though the availability of salmon is also mentioned in passing through the following trout locations.

Availability of Guides. In contrast to the North Island about ninety per cent of South Island guides are dry-fly operators and only ten per cent trolling specialists. However, guiding services are not so concentrated as in the north and guides are available throughout the island for a wide variety of fishing. Among locations discussed below, guides can be contacted at Christchurch, Lake Brunner, Wanaka, Queenstown, Te Anau, Gore, Lake McKerrow, Oamaru, Kurow, Tekapo and Rangitata for trips mainly in those areas. Guides

Angler fishing the Clinton River, familiar to walkers of the famous Milford Track. The Clinton flows into the head of Lake Te Anau and is reputed to be one of the best dry-fly streams in the world

who cater for the inexperienced 'thrill-type' angler as the launches do at Rotorua and Taupo are in the minority and mainly based at the towns of Te Anau, Wanaka and Queenstown. But as already indicated the majority of guides cater for experienced anglers of the dry-fly and nymph type.

SOUTHERN LAKES

This general region, protected to some extent from the prevailing westerlies by the Southern Alps and the mountains of Fiordland, comprises a series of major lakes—Wanaka and Hawea in the north, Wakatipu in the centre and, in the south, Te Anau, Manapouri, Monowai and Hauroko. Browns and rainbows are found in all lakes and streams, although some are predominantly brown. Landlocked salmon are found only in Lakes Hawea, Wanaka, Wakatipu, Te Anau and Manapouri. Throughout the region browns average 0.9–1.8 kg (2–4 lb), rainbows 0.9–1.4 kg (2–3 lb) and landlocked salmon 0.9 kg (2 lb). Browns of 2.3–2.7 kg (5–6 lb) are caught regularly and every year trout up to 3.6 or 4.5 kg (8 or 10 lb) are taken.

Access to the three main parts of the region is good from the three respective town centres, Wanaka, Queenstown and Te Anau. These three areas need to be looked at more closely as follows:

Wanaka and Hawea. For these two lakes trolling is the most popular method of fishing, and the many beaches and headlands provide excellent spinning and streamer-fly fishing for cruising trout. Dry-fly fishing is also productive during the summer months at Glendhu Bay, Wanaka, and at Highburn Swamp, Hawea.

The Makarora River and two side streams, the Wilkin and Young, enter the head of Lake Wanaka, while the Matukituki River flows into the lower lake from the west. These fast-flowing snow-fed streams fish well early or late in the season, with spinning, dry and wet fly tackle. The major feeder streams of Hawea are the Hunter, the Dingle and Timaru Creek, the first two being considered the best rivers in the entire district, holding browns and rainbows to 2.7 kg (6 lb). Proof of this is that the Hunter River was chosen by the Wildlife Service as the fishing location for Prince Charles on his recent visit to New Zealand. Prince Charles took five fish fly-fishing in the Hunter, four of them using a Turkey red or yellow and the fifth on a Kakahi Queen. All the above river mouths fish well from midsummer to the end of the season.

The outlets of both lakes, the Clutha River from Lake Wanaka and the Hawea River from Lake Hawea, provide good dry, wet and spinning down as far as their junction with the Lindis River. The dry fly here is highly recommended. Jetboats are mostly used for access to the Lower Makarora and Wilkin, as well as to the Hunter, Dingle, Timaru Creek and the Clutha. In addition there are a number of airstrips adjacent to the Makarora, Wilkin and Hunter, while the upper Dingle can be reached by helicopter.

Lake Wakatipu. Trolling on Lake Wakatipu, mainly with lead lines, is

(Opposite) *Falls and feeder stream at Diamond Lake in the lower Rees Valley at the head of Lake Wakatipu. Waters like this provide excellent dry-fly fishing*

157

most popular, especially on the western side and around Pig and Pidgeon Islands at the head of the lake. The stream mouths on the western side fish well with fly and nymph early and late in the season, and fly, nymph and spinner are all popular from the beaches and headlands for cruising trout. The mouths of the Greenstone, Dart and Rees rivers fish very well for landlocked salmon from February to April.

The notable feeder streams are the Lochy, Von, Greenstone and Caples rivers, which are all on the western side with access by boat across the lake. These all hold good populations of trout early and late in the season, and support big resident trout in the upper reaches. The Greenstone and its tributary, the Caples, are possibly two of the best fly-fishing streams in the district and in my view are among the best in the South Island, although of recent years, with helicopter access, both have been heavily fished. The other notable feeder streams reached by road from Glenorchy are the Dart and Rees rivers and Diamond Creek. The latter, though small, is one of the finest dry-fly streams to be found anywhere. The Kawarau River, the outlet to the lake, has very clear water and is difficult to fish but produces good spinning and fly water down as far as the Shotover junction; it is best fished by jetboat. If rain has discoloured most rivers in the district, the Kawarau usually stays clear for fishing.

There are seven smaller lakes handy to Queenstown, reached either by car or on foot, which contain rainbows, browns or both up to 1.4 kg (3 lb). These are Hayes, Johnson, Dispute, Luna, Reid, Diamond, Moke and Kilpatrick. Dry fly and nymph on all seven are the most productive methods.

Te Anau, Manapouri, Monowai, Hauroko. On Lakes Te Anau and Manapouri trolling is most popular, especially in the many sheltered arms and bays along their western shores, where of course there is no road access. Spinning in the same spots is also good, and dry-fly fishing most productive throughout the area. Some twenty-five rivers, streams and burns flow into these two lakes. Among those entering Te Anau are the Doon, Worsley, Clinton, Eglinton and Upukerora rivers, besides the Esk, Ettrick, Junction and Lugar burns. Lake Manapouri has the Grebe and Spey rivers as well as the Iris, Freeman and Ewe burns. In addition there is the very well-known Waiau River which connects the two lakes, providing about 15 kilometres of fishing water. Of those mentioned, the majority can only be reached by boat or float plane, notable exceptions being the Waiau, Upukerora and Eglinton, which have good road access. The Waiau is the most stable and therefore most popular, because it is less susceptible to flooding, although the other two provide very good dry-fly fishing early and late in the season. The Waiau is best fished using a jetboat, and provides excellent spinning, wet, nymph and dry-fly water. The Clinton and Worsley rivers, both usually very clear with large resident fish in their upper pools, offer some of the best fly fishing in the country.

Further south are Lakes Monowai and Hauroko, which have access roads as far as their shores but virtually nothing else, so fishing is mainly available to those with boats. Trolling, spinning, fly and nymph are all most productive on these very underfished lakes, with Monowai over the past few seasons producing trout, mainly from trolling, in the range 2.3–2.7 kg (5–6 lb).

Suggested lures and flies for all Southern Lakes and streams are: Spinners—Flatfish, Cobra, Slice, Minnow, Zed Spinner and Devon.

Angler fishing the confluence of the Young and Makarora rivers, two fine dry-fly streams which flow into Lake Wanaka

159

Dry Flies—Pevril O' Peak, Adams, Wulff, Light Cahill, Blue Dunn; also Spentwing, Cochy Bundu, Molefly and nymphs, all in sizes 10–14. Streamers—Mrs Simpson, Hamill's, Kilwell, in red, green and yellow.

SOUTHLAND—MATAURA RIVER

Southland is regarded as the dry-fly Mecca of New Zealand, with the Mataura River the most famous of all its waters. Indeed the whole region, with its profusion of over 2400 kilometres of stream banks and its high productivity, certainly lives up to this reputation. The trout are predominantly browns, averaging 0.9–1.4 kg (2–3 lb) but fish of 2.3–2.7 kg (5–6 lb) are caught regularly, and every year sees some in the range 3.2–4.1 kg (7–9 lb) taken. Dry fly and nymph fishing are most often employed and prove most productive but some wet fly can be used here and there and some waters are open to spinning.

The principal streams, reading from the far west, are the Whitestone (a tributary of the Waiau), Aparima and Oreti. Then comes the Mataura with its well known tributaries, the Nokomai, Waikaia, Waikaka, Waimea, Mimihau, Wyndham and Brightwater. Access is good to all of them, with roads either crossing or running parallel to the rivers. Ideal setting-out points are Gore for the lower reaches of the Mataura and tributaries, as well as for the famous 'mad rise' of the Mataura, Invercargill for the Oreti and Aparima, and Te Anau township for the upper reaches. Lakes in the region are the Mavora Lakes in the headwaters of the Mararoa (another tributary of the Waiau), which offer good fishing with either dry flies or spinners, and the Waituna Lagoon, Toetoes Bay, which is most productive of sea-run browns consistently of very large size.

All these waters fish best from November until Christmas and from February to April, with dry fly being most productive in the early morning or late evening, the long southern twilights being most favourable for the evening rise.

Suggested lures are: Dry flies—Adams, Goofus Bug, Royal Wulff, Blue Dunn, Pomahaka Black, Twilight Beauty, Dad's Favourite, Red-tipped Governor. Nymphs are most popular in sizes 10 to 18. Wet flies—Greenwell's Glory, Black Gnat, Twilight Beauty. Streamers—Matuka, Hamill's (red and green), Mrs Simpson, Kilwell.

An excellent publication, which fully describes the fishing waters, methods and times and has maps of all rivers, is available from the Southland Acclimatisation Society, P.O. Box 844, Invercargill.

This Southern Lakes-Southland region, plus perhaps the neighbouring Pomahaka River area in Otago (see page 164), remains

(Opposite) Landing a brown trout taken on a dry fly in the picturesque setting of South Mavora Lake, Western Southland

SOUTH ISLAND TROUT FISHING LOCATIONS

1 Motueka River system
2 Pelorus River
3 Wairau River
4 Clarence River
5 Waiau and Hurunui rivers
6 Waimakariri River
7 Rakaia River
8 Ashburton and Rangitata rivers
9 Waitaki River system
10 Taieri River
11 Clutha River system—and Roxburgh hydro lake
12 Pomahaka River
13 Mataura River system
14 Oreti River
15 Waiau River
16 Lakes Hauroko and Monowai
17 Lake Manapouri
18 Lake Te Anau
19 Eglinton River
20 Lake Wakatipu

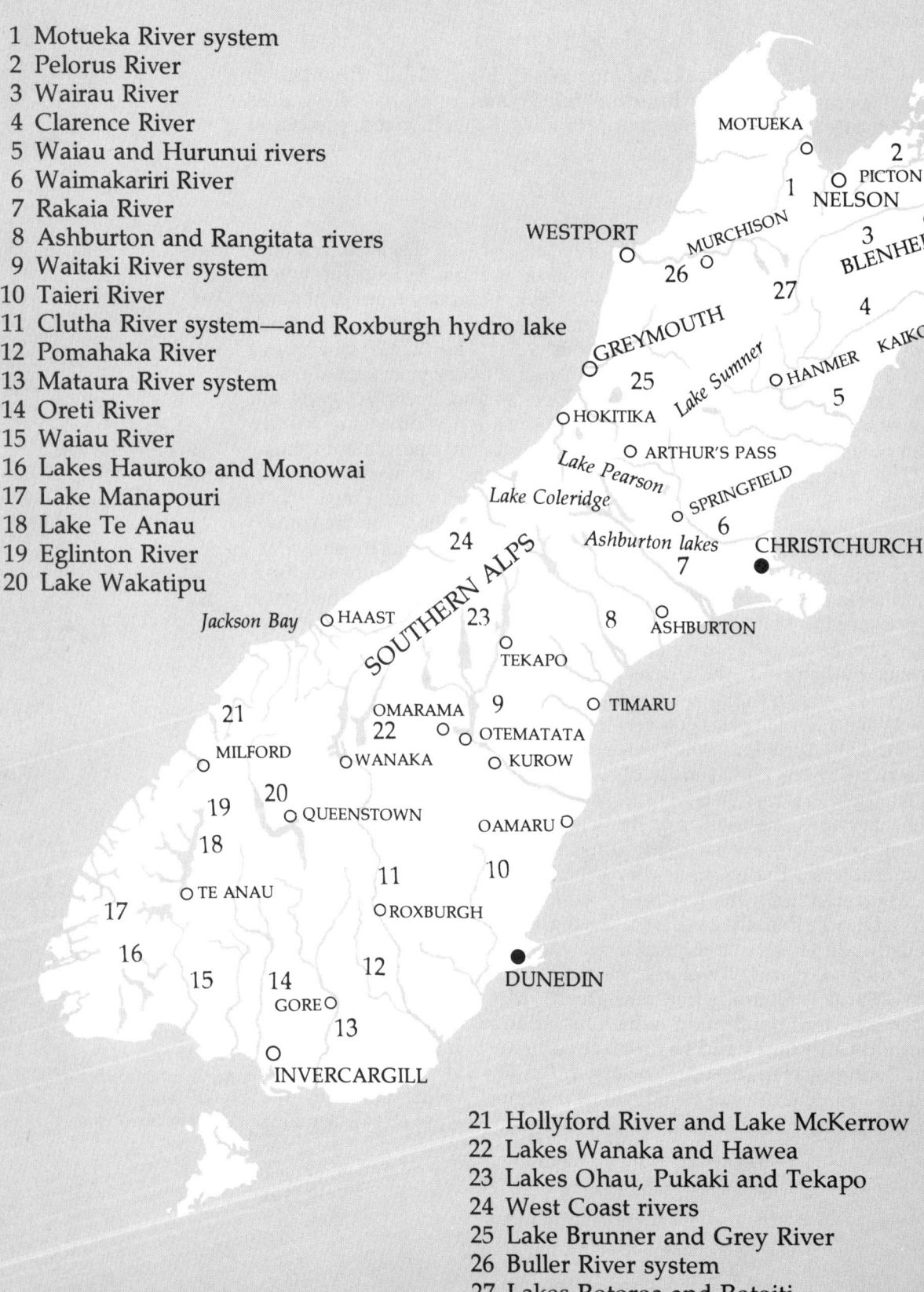

21 Hollyford River and Lake McKerrow
22 Lakes Wanaka and Hawea
23 Lakes Ohau, Pukaki and Tekapo
24 West Coast rivers
25 Lake Brunner and Grey River
26 Buller River system
27 Lakes Rotoroa and Rotoiti

my own favourite fishing destination in the south of the country. A few personal experiences and some told to me by overseas anglers may be of interest to other potential visitors, both local and tourist, who will certainly continue to be drawn to these parts. First thing that comes to mind for me is that it is not an area where one goes to catch large numbers of fish. In fact, a good dry-fly or nymph angler will consider himself lucky if he catches two good fish a day, and by good fish I mean those weighing 1.8–2.3 kg (4–5 lb). And to get those two he will usually have covered dozens of pools and have walked many kilometres up and down banks. As a comparison, in 1976 I fished a stretch of the Big Horn River, Montana, U.S.A., where the surroundings, the countryside and the river were very much like the Oreti in Southland. I have never experienced such action-packed fishing. For nearly an hour I was hooking a fish a cast, using a floating line and Royal Wulff dry fly. The fish I was taking were either Montana graylings or brook trout but the sad thing was they were all measuring about 25–30 cm (10–12 inches). Great fishing, but after New Zealand I would hesitate to call them fish. When fishing Southland and the Southern Lakes one seldom sees small fish like that but works harder to catch bigger, much bigger, fish. Not quantity but quality—that is the main difference.

In 1977 Tom Collins of Missoula, Montana, took two browns, each weighing 3.2 kg (7 lb), from the Oreti and in 1975 Walton Powell of Chico, California, caught a 3.6-kg (8-lb) brown there in my company, while making a TV movie. In 1977 Homer Peters of Albany, New York, took a 3.2-kg (7-lb) rainbow out of the Greenstone. Only last season an American called into my office to say that on his first day fishing the Whitestone he had hooked and landed a brown of 4.1 kg (9 lb)—his first trout in New Zealand. Naturally he thought he would have fishing like that all the time, so released the 9-pounder. To his disgust he never caught another as big during his stay and would have given his back teeth to have taken that first one home mounted. Anyway, these examples from a few of the weights I can recall will give an idea of the better quality (if not quantity) of fishing available.

Gore township is the ideal location to use as a base while fishing the Mataura, its central situation allowing forays both up and down the river. Croyden Lodge is a favourite hotel for anglers, and is situated on the outskirts of town. The chalets are spread around the grounds allowing you to drive the rental car right to the door. The lodge has a friendly bar, restaurant, and lunches are available for anglers. There are also a number of motels in Gore, if you prefer preparing your own meals.

Almost the patriarch of all Southland angling guides is also based in Gore, and who from angling clubs around the world hasn't heard of Peter

Cullen? Peter has now guided thousands of overseas fishermen on successful dry-fly fishing excursions throughout the region.

OTAGO

Within a 120-kilometre radius of Dunedin are some of the finest waters in the South Island for rainbows and browns. Besides the famous rivers and streams, there are Lakes Roxburgh, Onslow, Mahinerangi, Waipori and Waihola. There is also great variety in the water, from delightful little dry-fly streams to big rivers like the Clutha and estuary fishing for sea-run trout, giving the angler a range of methods, from dry and wet fly to spinning and live bait, rivalled by few other districts.

Starting in the south with the mighty Clutha, its main headwaters tributaries are the Lindis and Manuherikia rivers, and nearer the sea in South Otago it is joined by the Pomahaka and Waitahuna rivers and the Waiwera and Kaihiku streams. The Pomahaka is world renowned among anglers and along its whole 120 or so kilometres provides a profusion of excellent dry-fly water in which browns average 0.9–1.8 kg (2–4 lb). It has two tributary streams, the Waipahi and Wairuna. The Manuherikia on the upper Clutha fishes well for brown trout ranging from 0.5–1.8 kg (1–4 lb) and offers good stretches of wet, dry and spinning water.

Being wide and deep, the Clutha itself—and also the Roxburgh hydro lake—is preferred spinning water but does have good stretches for dry fly and nymphing. The river mouth affords very good fishing for sea-run browns using natural or artificial minnows.

Other rivers in the South Otago district are, from south, the Tahakopa, Catlins, Owaka, Puerua and Tokomairiro. All these provide good dry-fly and spinning water, although for smallish browns around 0.5 kg (1 lb). In the Catlins estuary trout up to 4.5 kg (10 lb) have been taken.

The Taieri River, like the Clutha, is another very long river, completing a tremendous arc round the Rock and Pillar Range to enter the sea south of Dunedin, near where it is joined by the Waipori and the waters from Lakes Mahinerangi, Waipori and Waihola. Other tributaries close to Dunedin are the Deep and Lee streams. The main river fishes best in its headwaters, where browns run from 0.9–1.8 kg (2–4 lb), with many up to 2.3 kg (5 lb) being taken annually. Deep and Lee are small streams with mainly small browns taken on dry fly or cricket. The Waipori provides very good dry-fly fishing in the upper reaches, mainly for browns in the 0.9-kg class (2 lb),

Nearly a metre long and weighing 8.9 kg (19½ lb), this brown trout was taken some years ago from the Waituna Lagoon, Toetoes Bay, Southland

although fish have been taken from Lake Mahinerangi to 4.5 kg (10 lb).

North of Dunedin are the Shag and Waikouaiti rivers in which browns from 0.5–1.4 kg (1–3 lb) are available. The former is a

165

preferred baitcasting waterway, while the latter fishes well with wet flies.

Most Otago waters fish well from October until Christmas and again in February and March. Recommended dry flies: Red-tipped Governor, Red Hackam, Red Quill, Dad's Favourite, Nimmo's Killer, Twilight Beauty, Pomahaka Red. Wet flies: Claret and Mallard, Turkey and Red, Red Matuka, Mrs Simpson. Spinners: Minnow, Devon, Loaded Cocoon, Wobblers. On some waters natural floating worm, cricket and minnow are most successful, though it is as well to check district regulations to see which rivers they may be used on.

WAITAKI WATERSHED

This extensive controlled system of waterways is now rapidly becoming one of the South Island's exciting angling regions. With brown trout and rainbows in the upper reaches, with both species plus salmon in the lower, with the variety it affords of stream, river and lake, and with its pretty reliable weather, it truly provides all that any angler could desire.

Within this system are the fishable lakes of Tekapo, Alexandrina, Pukaki, Ohau, Benmore, Aviemore and Waitaki, all of which provide trolling, spinning and good fly fishing for cruising trout. Fishing for resident fish is also good in the feeder streams and rivers to these lakes, especially Tekapo, Pukaki and Ohau. Other principal streams entering the river system are the Ahuriri, Otamatakau and Hakataramea, and these provide the best dry-fly fishing. On the lower reaches of the Waitaki, from the Waitaki dam to the sea, the hundreds of islands, mainly reached by jetboat, provide excellent spinning and fly fishing for all three species. Access is good to all waters from Tekapo in the north, from Omarama, Otematata and Kurow in the middle reaches, and from Oamaru at the lower end. Over the entire system the rainbows and browns average 0.9–1.4 kg (2–3 lb) but below the turbine outlets fish to 9.0 kg (20 lb) have been taken and others in the range 4.5–6.8 kg (10–15 lb) are caught regularly. The biggest in the 1977 season weighed 6.2 kg (13½ lb).

Suggested lures: Black, Silver or Blue Slice, Zed Spinner, Tinker, Tiger. Dry flies—Greenwell's Glory, Red-tipped Governor, Peveril O' Peak. Streamers—Mrs Simpson, Hope's Dark, Parsons' Glory, Yellow Dorothy.

WESTLAND

This region, stretching from Milford Sound in the south to Karamea in the north, is the most underfished in the entire country. Every river

166

carries fish, predominantly browns, but some have rainbows too, while quinnat salmon have been found in almost every river from the Taramakau to the Haast. Furthermore, the biggest migration of sea-run brown trout in New Zealand takes place in South Westland and Fiordland. The average weight of trout is 0.9–1.8 kg (2–4 lb)but sea-run browns have been averaging around 2.3 kg (5 lb). The most popular methods of fishing are spinning, nymph and dry fly.

The main reason this area is underfished is that many of the rivers travel only a short distance from mountains to sea, with a fast drop-off. They rise quickly in adverse weather and are susceptible to flooding and scouring. Any fisherman wishing to make a success of his angling in this general location needs a reliable source of weather information.

Starting from the far south, the Westland region can best be dealt with in three main areas.

Fiordland. A road into Milford Sound from Te Anau gives access to the lower Cleddau River, which provides good but limited fishing for sea-run browns in its lower reaches. From Milford it is possible to cross the sound by launch and then walk up part of the Milford Track to reach Lake Ada and the Arthur and Joe rivers, although a helicopter when available at Milford simplifies access. Best fishing here is after a fresh or in dry periods, and trout are not very selective in choice of fly or lure. They are most prolific, however, affording some of the best fishing in South Westland, with browns running 1.8–2.7 kg (4–6 lb).

There is no road access to the lower Hollyford and Pike rivers, where the famous Lakes McKerrow, Alabaster and Wilmot are situated, but one can fly in from Queenstown or Te Anau, or take several days to walk and camp. There is a fishing lodge situated at the sea end of Lake McKerrow. This fishing is similar to Milford Sound fishing, equally as good, but with more water available. The area is fished best from September to Christmas, and then again in March and April. Like Milford, spinning, dry or wet fly are equally successful for browns in the range 1.8–2.7 kg (4–6 lb).

The fishing season in the Fiordland region opens on the first of September so that anglers can take advantage of the sea-run migration of brown trout. This run also coincides with the annual migration of whitebait, the season for netting which also opens on 1 September. The sea-run browns follow the whitebait into the river mouths, where they delight in a frenzy of feeding on this succulent delicacy, so can easily be taken with any imitation whitebait lure or fly. The North Island lakes' fly, the Grey Ghost, is an excellent imitation of a whitebait and is most successful, as is any spinning lure

Nowadays jetboats are used pretty extensively for angling access on South Island rivers–as here on the Waitaki

of similar size and shape such as a Toby or Zed Spinner. An interesting sidelight is that in the old days whitebaiters hated these trout, as they considered they chased the whitebait away from their nets, so they paid boys a bounty to take trout by any available means and hundreds were killed for this reason. No doubt in some areas the practice still continues, although needless to say it is frowned upon by both sportsmen and wildlife authorities. The biggest sea-run brown I have heard of in recent years from this area was a 5.0-kg (11-lb) trout taken in Lake McKerrow.

After following the whitebait in, the browns mostly stay in holding areas like Lake McKerrow and Lake Ada, before moving on up rivers like the Arthur and the Hollyford to spawn later in the year. When they first come in from the sea, they are silver like quinnat salmon or deep-lake rainbows, and of course fat and in excellent condition, having recently gorged on whitebait. However, once upstream and intent on spawning, like rainbows and salmon they go off food, but can be tempted with dry flies and nymphs.

This area is underfished like the rest of Westland and will probably remain that way for a long time to come. For that reason it will always provide excellent fishing. Access is not easy, and as well there is the insect problem, which does more than anything else to keep anglers out of the area. Sandflies and mosquitoes, the latter of the four-engined variety, just love unlocalised blood and descend in hordes. The targets swell in lumps and are irritated by constant scratching. A good supply of insect repellent is a must in this location.

Central and South Westland (Greymouth to Jackson Bay). Road access is good in this area. Coming from south, the highway through the alps follows the Haast River from source to sea and then, turning north as the coast road, intersects every river from Haast township to Greymouth. There is similar main-road access to most of the Taramakau River and to the Grey River system.

Every river crossed has fish in it, and these are best fished early in the season between the coast road bridge and the sea. Upstream pools on the longer rivers hold resident fish and these can be fished all summer. Spinning is more popular on the lower reaches, with dry fly preferred in the upper. These are all whitebait rivers, and any imitation such as the Toby wobbler or Grey Ghost streamer fly will have good success in the lower reaches early in the season.

In the upper reaches of the longer rivers, especially in South Westland south of Haast, venison export hunters have built many airstrips for light planes and these are proving a bonus in opening up many remote unfished areas to anglers, making it an angler-explorer paradise. Notable larger rivers from north to south are the Grey

169

system, the Taramakau, Arahura, Hokitika system, Wanganui (and its tributary La Fontaine Stream), Whataroa, Cook, Karangarua, Paringa and Haast. In addition there are Lakes Brunner, Kaniere, Ianthe, Mapourika, Paringa and Moeraki. South of the Haast River turnoff there are the Okuru, Turnbull, Waiatoto and Arawata rivers, each of which has venison-loading airstrips at intervals along its length.

The two top dry-fly waters of Westland have always been considered the Arnold River, a tributary of the Grey flowing out of Lake Brunner, and the shortish, spring-fed La Fontaine Stream at Harihari. The Arnold produces good browns to 1.4 kg (3 lb), the La Fontaine browns slightly smaller on average, though trout up to 2.7 kg (6 lb) have been taken. The two waterways have something in common in that neither is snow-fed like most Westland rivers, so that they remain relatively clear when others are often unfishable.

All over this part of Westland there is a wealth of virtually untouched dry-fly fishing available, particularly when one thinks of such waters as the tributaries of the Taramakau, Lake Moeraki and the rivers south of the Haast. As regards lake waters, Brunner, the largest, is considered the best fishing lake in Westland. It fishes equally well with dries, wets, spinners and 'live' bully baits. Its dry-fly feeder streams are the Orangipuku and Crooked rivers; in addition, dry fly is most productive along the lake edge. Trout here are averaging 0.9–1.8 kg (2–4 lb), but every year trout up to 3.6 kg (8 lb) are taken. There is a fishing lodge at Mitchells on the lake edge.

Deerhunters tell endless stories of large trout in never-fished holes in remote Westland rivers. There are certainly plenty of places where it is rare to see another angler, and for some this is the main attraction of the area.

The Buller Watershed. The Buller River rises in the northern tip of the Southern Alps in the Travers River, which flows into Lake Rotoiti, and the Sabine and D'Urville rivers flowing into Lake Rotoroa. The outlets of the two lakes then join, forming the main Buller River which makes its way to the West Coast, entering the sea at Westport. On its way to the sea the main tributaries joining it are the Owen, Mangles, Matakitaki, Maruia and Inangahua, the latter having as its main side stream the notable Larrys Creek. Access is good to all waters, as the Westport-Murchison road follows the main river and the northern reaches are gained from the Murchison-Nelson road.

The chief method of fishing in the main river is using spinning gear or dry fly, but dry fly and nymph are more successful in all the tributaries. Some of the best fishing in the area is in the Travers, Sabine and D'Urville, which can only be reached by boat across the

One of the finest dry-fly streams in Westland—the La Fontaine Stream at Harihari

respective lakes, and then by walking up each. Trout here average 1.8 kg (4 lb) but fish up to 5 kg (11 lb) have been taken. The two lakes fish well with both spinning gear and dry fly or nymph from boats or the shore. The main river, although easily accessible and heavily fished, produces trout averaging 0.9–1.8 kg (2–4 lb) and is a consistent fish producer and an attractive dry-fly river.

Suggested flies and lures for all Westland are: Dry flies—Blue Dunn, March Brown, Black Gnat, Kakahi Queen, Wulff, Adam's. Smelt patterns—Mrs Simpson, Hamill's red and green, Red Shadow, Green Smelt, Kilwell, Grey Ghost. Spinners—Minnow, Devon, Cobra, Toby, Slice, Zed Spinner.

NELSON-MARLBOROUGH

Nelson provides some of the finest dry-fly waters in the South Island with such famous rivers as the Takaka, Riwaka, Motueka, Wairoa, Pelorous, Wairau, Opawa, and its greatest remote attraction, the Karamea. This latter is renowned for producing brown trout to 3.6 kg (8 lb). There is also top fishing on lakes Rotoiti and Rotoroa with the latter having the attractive Rotoroa Lodge on its shores, a popular angling destination for local and overseas anglers. The lodge provides access by boat to the remote D'Urville and Sabine rivers which flow into the head of the lake and produce some excellent dry-fly fishing. As well, the lodge is situated right on the banks of the Gowan River and only a few miles by road to the mid-reaches of the famous Buller River.

In Marlborough are the three notable big rivers, the Wairau, Awatere and Clarence, all holding a good head of browns, although rainbows have recently been released in the latter. The browns from all three have been averaging 1.8 kg (4 lb) and the Clarence regularly produces fish in the 2.2–2.7 kg (5–6 lb) class. Access is good to the former from Blenheim, but the latter only has good access from the coast road to the lower reaches, or road access to the upper from Hanmer. The middle reaches would have to be walked and camped, or reached by helicopter.

Flies and lures are the same as for Westland.

NORTH CANTERBURY

Principal waters in this area are the Waiau, Hurunui, Waimakariri, Ashley and Rakaia rivers, and the three groups of high-country lakes, related respectively to Lakes Sumner, Pearson and Coleridge, plus Lake Ellesmere on the east coast. The Waiau is fished from Parnassus in its lower reaches, principally for salmon, but holds good brown trout in the upper, while, adjacent to Hanmer, the Hope and Boyle tributaries hold both browns and rainbows. Likewise, the Rakaia and Waimakariri are principally salmon rivers, but also hold good trout in the upper reaches, with the latter being possibly the best trout river, having both rainbows and browns in its upper reaches. They both have good road access, the latter especially being reached easily from the Christchurch-Arthur's Pass highway. Light spinning tackle is most favoured, although dry fly and nymph is productive early morning and late evening. Rainbows and browns have been averaging 0.9–1.4 kg (2–3 lb), but fish up to about 2.7 kg (6 lb) have been taken regularly over recent seasons. The Waimakariri is readily accessible to the best fishing locations by jetboat.

The high-country lakes are well worth fishing as they hold browns, rainbows or both, running from 0.5–1.8 kg (1–4 lb) depending on the lake. However, regulations should be studied as some are 'fly only', others provide both fly and spinning. The northern group of small lakes centring on Lake Sumner is reached by an inland road turning off State Highway 7 at Waikari. All the lakes in the other two groups are reached either on the Springfield-Arthur's Pass road (Highway 73) or by turning off this road at Lake Lyndon. All lakes are exposed to the winds, but access around them for shore fishing is very good. Lake Ellesmere holds brown trout and fishes best at the mouths of the Selwyn and Halswell rivers, although a boat to fish from is recommended.

Flies and lures are the same as for South Canterbury (see below).

ASHBURTON-SOUTH CANTERBURY

Principal waters are the Ashburton, Hinds, Rangitata, Orari, Opihi and Pareora rivers and the high-country lakes. The Ashburton and Rangitata are principally salmon waters, though they hold resident browns and sea-run browns in the lower reaches and large resident browns up to 3.2 kg (7 lb) in the upper reaches. In the upper Rangitata particularly, streams on either side on Mesopotamia and Mount Potts stations have been producing browns up to that same weight in the past few seasons.

Possibly the best river system in the district is the Opihi, which has the Temuka, Waihi, Tengawai and Hae Hae Te Moana streams as tributaries. These are all easily accessible from Temuka or Geraldine. The trout in this system have been averaging 0.5–1.4 kg (1–3 lb), with fish taken below the junction of the Temuka and Opihi rivers often running as high as 3.6 kg (8 lb). The Opihi system is ideal for dry-fly or

173

nymph fishing in the early morning or late evening, also during the midday hours, and at its lower end, particularly at its mouth, the river is one of the best salmon rivers in Canterbury.

The back-country 'Ashburton lakes'—Heron, Emma, Clearwater, Emily, Camp, Spider, Denny, Maori and Roundabout—all hold fish and are 'fly only', except Heron, Camp and Roundabout. Lake Emily is stocked with *fontinalis* trout; other lakes hold browns, rainbows or both. Trout are mainly in the 0.5–0.9 kg range (1–2 lb) but Lake Heron has regularly produced fish between 2.3 and 2.7 kg (5 and 6 lb).

Suggested flies and lures are: Dry flies—Blue Dunn, Dad's Favourite, March Brown, Black Gnat, Kakahi Green, green and brown beetle and nymphs. Smelt patterns—Mrs Simpson, Hamill's red and yellow, Kilwell.

SALMON FISHING

In New Zealand salmon are found only in the South Island, where two species, the Atlantic salmon and the Pacific salmon known as quinnat, are acclimatised. The former is now almost certainly landlocked, while the latter is both landlocked and sea-run.

ATLANTIC SALMON

These salmon, introduced over many years, are now only to be found in the water systems of Lakes Manapouri and Te Anau, with the biggest population occurring in Lakes Gunn and Fergus, headwaters lakes of the Eglinton River, a feeder of Lake Te Anau. Possibly most are taken by anglers in the Waiau River, which connects Lakes Te Anau and Manapouri, as this is the most heavily fished river in the area, and are taken by anglers usually fishing for browns or rainbows. However, anyone wishing to fish exclusively for Atlantics would be well advised to try Lakes Gunn and Fergus.

An interesting sidelight on the successful 1908 liberation of this species is that it was then hoped they would expand into the rivers of Fiordland and become the basis of a million-dollar industry to rival the salmon fishery of the American northwest. However, to confound the experts it seems that the species, on liberation, failed to migrate to sea. Instead, there is evidence now that they spawn in the rivers and mature in the lakes. At the same time, little research has so far been done on this salmon in New Zealand.

The most successful method of catching them has been trolling,

(Opposite) *Mokihinui River, a prolific but little fished dry-fly stream on the west coast of Nelson Province*

175

usually with a minnow or with a small articulated trout lure or a small Zed Spinner. The average weight of salmon caught has been around 0.9 kg (2 lb), although in 1976 one weighing 1.8 kg (4 lb) was taken in Lake Gunn.

QUINNAT SALMON

These are the most common salmon available here and grow the largest of all our freshwater sport fishes. In the northwest of the United States and British Columbia they are known as chinook, king or spring salmon, with the very big ones over 20 kg (45 lb) called Tyee salmon. In the South Island quinnats are found on both the east and west coasts, where they come back from the sea usually as three-year-olds to spawn, but they are also landlocked in Lakes Hawea, Wanaka and Wakatipu.

Where they are landlocked these salmon average 0.9–1.4 kg (2–3 lb) and can be taken at stream mouths through the summer on nymphs or wet flies, but as a rule most landlocked salmon are taken on spinning lures such as tice, minnows and the Zed Spinner. I have had my best success with spinners at the mouths of streams in March when the salmon are preparing to run upstream to spawn. I once spent a very pleasant afternoon at the mouth of the Greenstone on Lake Wakatipu with Ted Trueblood, the veteran angling writer for *Field and Stream* magazine. We had tried all sorts of flies with no success, although the fish were there in large numbers, as they could be seen all over the place just breaking the surface with their noses. Ted tied on a nymph and put on a floating line with a sink tip. The results were immediate—one brown, one rainbow and one land-locked salmon, all taken on the same fly and all weighing around 1.4 kg (3 lb). Experimenting of that kind at all the stream mouths such as the Rees, Dart and Greenstone on Lake Wakatipu, the Matukituki and Makarora on Lake Wanaka and the Hunter and Dingle on Lake Hawea will almost certainly prove successful.

East Coast. The main salmon rivers of the South Island are on the east coast and from north to south are the Waiau, Hurunui, Waimakariri, Rakaia, Ashburton, Rangitata, Opihi and Waitaki. All of these rivers have good road access to their mouths on the sea coast and all have similar access, often up either side, for most of their fishable length. Anglers prefer fishing these waters when the runs are on, often from as early as December to as late as the end of April, although the best time is from mid-February on into April. It should be noted, however, that many of the upstream sections of most rivers close at the end of February to allow spawning to take place undisturbed.

A great many South Island anglers prefer fishing for quinnats at the river mouths, using surf-casting rods and spinning lures in the surf. So popular is this sport that when the runs are starting there is often standing room only along the beaches. They comprise some of the heaviest concentrations of anglers I have seen anywhere in the country.

Once the salmon have started upstream, like spawning trout they go off feeding and are most difficult to take. But upstream is where the challenge and the most pleasant fishing is to be found. Most of these shingle rivers split into numerous channels, forming hundreds of islands as streams divide and rejoin and adding up to thousands of pools and salmon lies. Using waders, anglers can get out to most islands as long as the rivers are not in flood, but by far the best means of access is the jetboat. Upstream anglers still use spinning rods or baitcasting rods with spoons or spinning lures such as the Zed Spinner (most popular in the large size) or the slice and Colorado Spinner (often used in conjunction with 15–30 gram weight). However, of recent years fly anglers have started using the Tongariro-type shooting-head lines in conjunction with a stripping basket and streamer flies such as the Red Setter, Hamill's and Mrs Simpson. The success they have had with this rig has opened up tremendous fishing opportunities for fly anglers.

The average weight of salmon taken is around 5.4 kg (12 lb) but plenty of fish are caught weighing up to 9.0 kg (20 lb) and every year one hears of fish being taken up to 18 kg (40 lb).

In February 1977 a friend of mine, Keith Williams of Auckland, who had never fished for salmon before, went down to the South Island for a week's fishing on the Rangitata River. He took eight fish ranging from 5.4 kg (12 lb) up to 9.9 kg (22 lb). This will give some idea of the size of fish that can be expected.

West Coast. Very little research has been carried out on the West Coast salmon runs. In fact, almost nothing was known of them before the completion of the Haast Pass road. However, salmon have been found in most rivers between and including the Taramakau and the Haast, and in 1975 stripping was carried out for the first time in the Paringa River for further liberations. So we can look forward to a future of good salmon fishing in this region, and anyone with the time to explore has an exciting challenge open to him. To assist with re-establishment, parts of Westland are closed to salmon fishing, so a study of the regulations is recommended before embarking on a salmon-fishing trip. Methods same as for the east coast.

177

Cooking
and
Smoking Trout

I have never talked much about my prowess as a cook. In fact, I am rather reticent on the subject, for in the years when I ran hunting and fishing safaris a friend once remarked, 'When Forrester cooks, even the bloody gravy is tough.' But trout I can cook, especially over an open fire, when it is at its best—and when the out-of-doors will have done something for the appetite. Naturally, therefore, I recommend the outdoor recipes. Once you have caught your trout, a simple and good outdoor method of cooking it will put the finishing touches to an already perfect day.

WHICH TROUT SHOULD YOU EAT?

Most experienced anglers know a good trout when they see one, just as a farmer can pick a fat lamb for the table. Those, however, who don't know what constitutes a good trout are advised to study the condition-factor chart opposite, which is what most anglers use to measure the quality of their catch. Among anglers, of course, there exists the inevitable 'give away' set-up or procedure, which means they give away to mothers-in-law, distant relations and such the worst of their catch and keep the best for home consumption. In my earlier book, *Hunting in New Zealand*, I drew attention to this practice among deer shooters and warned readers to be 'wary of venison that's given to you'. When a chap goes hunting he may only shoot one animal and it may be a twenty-year-old stag—and you wouldn't buy a twenty-year-old sheep from choice, even if you could. The same applies to trout, or at least to gifts of trout received. . . . Anyway, it all adds up to the fact that if you want a good trout for eating hot off the pan, you had best go out and catch one for yourself.

A good trout will have a high condition factor, preferably over fifty (see chart) and the higher the better. It will be fat, short and stocky and preferably a maiden (unspawned) or young fish, although age doesn't really matter if the condition factor is high. A good trout will keep its condition for several hours, but a poor one will soon show its hollow slabby belly. Be wary, therefore, of a long thin fish; it will generally be in poor condition.

If your trout is short and plump and when you turn it upside down a while after catching it doesn't look hollow-bellied, then the chances are that when you open it up to clean it the flesh will be red. Remember that salmon from the sea are judged for quality by their colour—the redder they are the better. The same applies to trout. A white-fleshed trout is usually a poor one to eat, with very little flavour. When a trout has been upstream spawning, it usually has not eaten for weeks and its strenuous love-making activities have used

180

TROUT CONDITION FACTORS -- GENERAL TABLES

WEIGHT IN GRAMS

Length (cm)	450	675	900	1125	1350	1575	1800	2025	2250	2475	2700	2925	3150	3375	3600	3825	4050	4275	4500	4725	4950	5175	5400	5625	5850	6075	6300	6525	6750	Length (in)
30	60	90																												12
31	54	81																												
32	49	74	99																											
33	45	67	90																											13
34	41	62	82																											
35	37	56	75	94																										
36	34	52	69	87																										
37	32	48	64	80	96																									
38	29	44	59	74	88																									15
39	27	41	54	68	82	95																								
40	25	38	50	63	76	88																								
41	23	35	47	58	70	82	94																							
42	21	32	43	54	65	76	87	98																						
43	20	30	40	51	61	71	81	92																						17
44		28	38	47	57	66	76	85	95																					
45		26	35	44	53	62	71	80	89	98																				
46		25	33	41	50	58	66	75	83	91																				
47		23	31	39	46	54	62	70	78	86	93																			
48		22	29	36	44	51	58	66	73	80	88																			19
49		20	27	34	41	48	55	62	69	76	82	89	96																	
50			26	32	39	45	52	58	65	71	78	84	91																	
51			24	30	36	42	49	55	61	67	73	79	85	91																20
52			23	28	34	40	46	52	57	63	69	75	80	85																
53			21	27	32	38	43	49	54	60	65	70	76	81	87	92														
54			20	25	30	36	41	46	51	56	61	67	72	77	82	87														
55				24	29	34	39	43	48	53	58	63	68	73	78	83	87	92												
56				23	27	32	37	41	46	50	55	60	64	69	74	78	83	87	92	97										22
57				21	26	30	35	39	43	48	52	57	61	65	70	74	79	83	87	92										
58				20	24	29	33	37	41	45	49	54	58	62	66	70	74	79	83	87	91	95								
59					23	27	31	35	39	43	47	51	55	59	63	67	71	75	79	83	87	91								
60					22	26	30	33	37	41	45	48	52	56	60	63	67	71	75	79	82	86	90							
61					21	25	28	32	35	39	42	46	50	53	57	60	64	68	71	75	78	82	85							24
62					20	23	27	30	34	37	40	44	47	51	54	57	61	64	68	71	75	78	81	85	89					
63						22	26	29	32	35	39	42	45	48	52	55	58	61	65	68	71	74	78	81	85	88				
64						21	24	27	31	34	37	40	43	46	49	52	55	58	62	65	68	71	74	77	80	83	86	89		
65						20	23	26	29	32	35	38	41	44	47	50	53	56	59	62	65	68	71	73	76	79	82	85		
66						22	25	28	31	33	36	39	42	45	48	50	53	56	59	62	65	67	70	73	76	79	81	84		26

WEIGHT IN POUNDS (APPROX): ½ POUND INTERVALS — pound markers: 1 2 3 4 5 6 7 8 9 10 11 12 13 14 15

Length in centimetres

By courtesy of the Wildlife Service N.Z. Dept. of Internal Affairs

Length in inches (approx.)

up all its reserves of fat. It will return to the lake in very poor condition, the flesh will be white in colour, the body long and thin, and in this state they are referred to as 'slabs' or 'kelts'. Good anglers usually return these fish alive to the water so that they can rebuild condition. They should never be eaten. They could put you off trout for life.

When a tourist catches such a fish it can be a considerable embarrassment to the guide. It may be the only fish the inexperienced tourist lands and he will be impressed with its length and immediately have visions of seeing it brought to the table on a silver platter, complete with trimmings, to feed the rest of his tour party. The guide doesn't have the heart to tell him that it's a lousy specimen and many is the shamefaced guide I have seen trying to smuggle such a fish into a tourist hotel without being spotted. Of course most guides usually have good trout in the freezer they can substitute and experienced chefs also know how to do the 'switcheroo'—but the situation can be embarrassing.

Author's son Gary with a 4.5 kg (10 lb) female rainbow from Lake Tarawera. Note the very high condition factor of this specimen

182

Poor trout are more prevalent at the beginning of the season before they have had the time to build up condition during the summer. Visiting American anglers set an excellent example by returning all trout to the water except for one good eater. If we were to follow their example we too could assist conservation and ensure sport for future generations.

CLEANING TROUT

It is not good policy to leave trout uncleaned for any length of time. I prefer to clean those destined for the table as soon as possible. The following method of cleaning trout is fast and simple, and once you get the hang of it you will probably use it for the rest of your life.

First make a cut under the lower jaw big enough to be able to insert your thumb and hook it round the lower jaw (Fig. 1). Next make a cut from the anus to the gills (Fig. 2). These are the only two cuts required. Hook the thumb of one hand round the lower jaw and with the other hand take a firm grip on the gills, getting your middle finger right round the gills to the backbone. Pull firmly with the hand grasping the gills, allowing your middle finger to follow the backbone (Fig. 3).

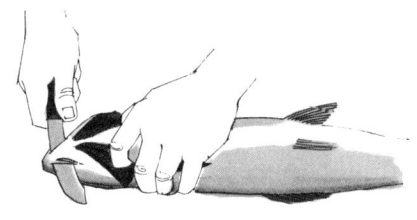

Figure 1. First cut for removing gut and gills.

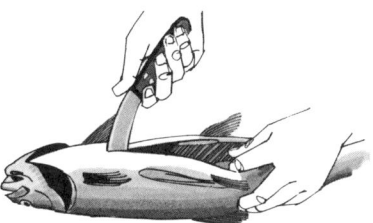

Figure 2. Second cut—continue cut to meet first cut.

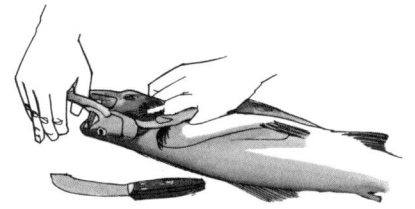

Figure 3. With thumb of one hand in jaw, grasp gills with the other hand and pull. Gills and gut will be removed in one operation.

183

Roger Forrester, a popular Rotorua fishing guide, preparing barbeque trout for clients on a lakeside beach

This pull will remove the entrails, the gills and the two pectoral fins, and on small trout, if you keep your middle finger firmly against the backbone, you will remove the liver as well, all in a single operation. However, if the trout is a large one, you will have to remove the liver separately and a teaspoon makes an ideal implement for this. If you don't have one, split the liver from end to end with a knife and scrape it out. It is essential to remove all traces of liver, gills and blood as they will hasten spoilage. The fish can then be washed and placed in a plastic bag until required for cooking. Leaving the head on makes the trout still attractive for photos, even after cleaning by this method.

WEIGHT LOSS

Many anglers do not like to clean their trout until they have them officially weighed, though this usually applies to competitions or pretty large specimens.

The table below will give some idea of how much weight a fish will lose over periods of six and twelve hours.

Initial weight		Weight after 6 hours			Weight after 12 hours		
kg	lb	kg	lb	oz	kg	lb	oz
0.45	1	0.44		15½	0.43		15
1.80	4	1.73	3	13	1.70	3	12
4.54	10	4.31	9	8	4.26	9	6

It will be seen that the weight loss tapers off and is greater over the first six hours. Over a twelve-hour period it is still only of the order of 560 grams per kilo or one ounce per lb and it makes you wonder if it is worth spoiling the trout for a few grams or ounces. Are records all that important?

FILLETING TROUT

First remove the head and place the trout upside down on a bread or fish board. You will need a very sharp knife to make a cut from the inside of the trout along the line made by the rib ends. With the knife edge between the ribs and the flesh, cut right down until the backbone is reached (Fig. 4). You will strike a few bones here but with a little force you will be able to cut through these out to the back (Fig. 5). Do the same on each side and you finish up with two fillets relatively bone free, as you will have done away with the entire backbone, rib cage and tail, which should be all in one piece.

These fillets can be cut into pan-size portions still with the skin on if you choose, as scales do not flake off as they do from sea fish. Indeed,

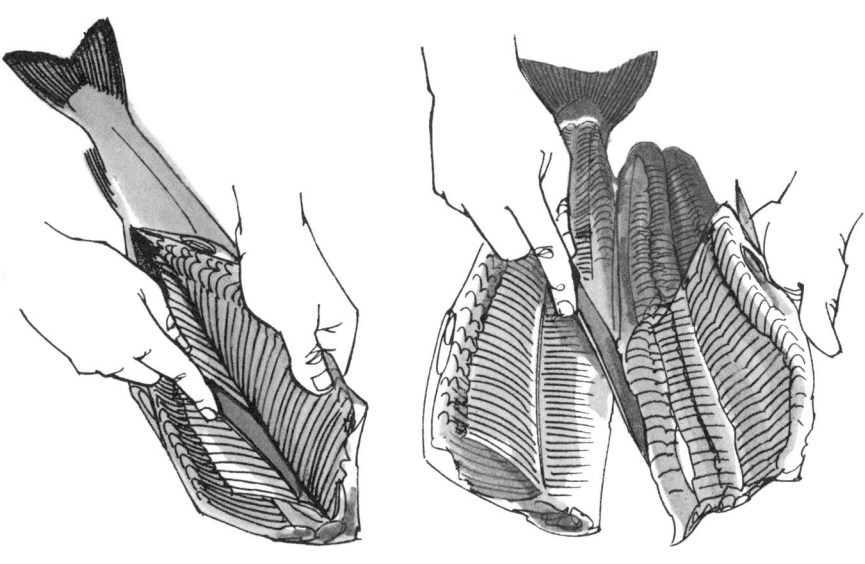

Figure 4. After removing the head and the liver along the backbone, run knife down between flesh and rib cage to remove fillet from either side.

Figure 5. Fillet is removed, leaving most of the bones attached to the skeleton.

185

for some methods of cooking, such as in a Kilwell smoker, it is as well to leave the skin on. For pan frying or fondue cooking, however, the trout is much better with the skin removed.

The skin can be removed without much trouble. Place a fillet, skin side down, on a flat board and always start from the tail end. Carefully cut between skin and flesh until you have enough skin exposed to grasp hold of. Grasp this skin with one hand and with the other hold the knife flat, blade facing forward and forced hard down against the skin. Pull evenly with the hand holding the skin and the skin will come away cleanly and surprisingly easily (Fig. 6). You can then cut the fillets into smaller portions or store in freezer bags until required.

Figure 6. Insert knife between skin and flesh, grasp skin with other hand and pull to remove skin from fillet.

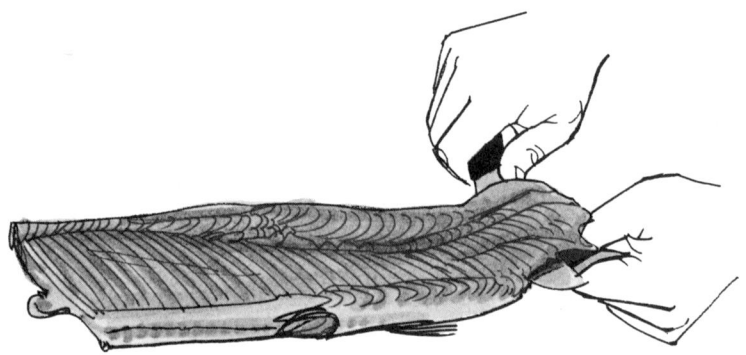

INDOOR COOKING—PAN-FRIED TROUT

This is possibly the most used method of cooking trout and is best when the trout are cooked the same day as they are caught.

First skin the fillets and cut into pan-size portions, rub a little lemon into each portion and sprinkle liberally with salt. Dip each, first into milk, then into a saucer of flour and place them in the pan already simmering with hot butter and fry until cooked or nicely browned. Do not overcook, but just make sure that each portion is cooked through. A few slices of onion in the pan will add to the flavour. The fillets can then be garnished with a little parsley and served best with french fries and slices of lemon.

FONDUE TROUT

My family have become very keen on fondue cooking over the past few years and recently when my son caught a fat young Tarawera

186

trout we decided to cook it, à la fondue, the same evening. I filleted and skinned the trout and cut it into fondue-sized cubes and while the pan of safflower oil was heating on the stove, decided to marinate the trout in vinegar. I placed a cupful of vinegar in a bowl and placed the cubes into this, after first liberally sprinkling with salt. The cubes could then be skewered on to the forks and cooked in the oil in the normal fondue style and eaten with a salad. Needless to say it was mouth-watering and this method can lead to a lot of experimentation with marinations and sauces. I am sure you will enjoy your trout cooked in this fashion.

BAKED OR STEAMED TROUT

This method of cooking a trout is designed as a main meal, and is ideal for a trout that has been kept for a few days in a fridge or longer in a freezer. The head can be left on, so that it can be brought to the table all complete on a silver tray, but in most cases cut the head off. Always leave the tail on the fish, as I shall explain later. The stomach cavity should be filled with stuffing, mainly to your own choice, but the following ingredients are fine: Enough breadcrumbs to fill the stomach cavity, a small clove of garlic, a large onion, butter and a teaspoon of mixed herbs. Chop up the onion and garlic and place in a pan of butter to cook—use just enough butter. When the onions are cooked, pour in the breadcrumbs and mixed herbs and mould all into a ball that will fit into the stomach cavity. The butter will bind the breadcrumbs and hold them together. You do not need to sew up the cavity as the wrapping will hold the stuffing in place. Wrap tightly in baking foil to make an airtight parcel and bake in a hot oven, usually 200–220°C, for from 15–20 minutes, depending on the size of the trout.

When the trout is cooked, you will be able to take hold of the tail and lift gently and the whole backbone and rib cage with skin attached will come away, leaving only the cooked flesh with relatively few bones to bother you. Spread with butter, garnish with parsley and serve with boiled potatoes and salad. You will find this an excellent way to cook trout as it will be steamed in its own juices.

OUTDOOR COOKING METHODS

If you are spending a day on a stream, or coming ashore from a boat, cooking a trout over an open fire can add to your pleasures. Most fishing areas of New Zealand have a plentiful supply of manuka wood, which is excellent for cooking fires as it produces hot coals and gives off a pleasant aroma. Just the fact that you are occupied in a pleasant outdoor activity gives you an appetite, and this combined with manuka smoke and the smell of sizzling trout really gets the taste buds working.

Pan-frying and steaming trout indoors both have their outdoor equivalent methods. They are simpler, not having a well-stocked kitchen at your disposal, but the simplicity, the aromas and the pleasant surroundings to my mind make them better.

GRILLED TROUT

If you are packing along a lunch on a fishing trip, then by all means throw in a spare pound of butter, a couple of onions and a salt shaker. These are the only ingredients you will need—bar the trout, of course—to grill a trout outdoors. If you have the room, such as in a boat, then it helps to have a griller along to save you making one, and a roll of greaseproof paper will do for plates. If you don't have a griller, then one can be made from fencing wire or chicken netting and supported over the coals on a couple of green saplings.

First build a good fire of manuka logs, adding a few green logs which will make the hottest coals, and place some rocks or logs on either side of the fire to support the griller. Once you have a good heap of red-hot coals, take away any wood that is still burning and you are ready to start grilling.

Clean the trout and cut the head off, but leave the tail and skin attached. With your knife cut from the inside into the backbone so that the trout can be laid out flat like an open book. You can then lay it on the griller, skin side down over the coals. I usually have the griller about 150 centimetres (six inches) above the coals, but you can raise it or lower it according to the heat. Liberally sprinkle the trout with salt and slice the onion into thin rings and lay these all over the top side. As the trout cooks, the onion and salt will permeate down into the flesh adding their flavour, while the manuka smoke from the outside will be adding aroma and colouring. When it is nearly cooked, and you can test this by cutting into the trout with a knife, gently turn the trout over so that the top side can brown up to your taste. Do not worry about the onions falling off when you do this as they will have done their job. Remove the trout to a piece of greaseproof paper (or a plate if you have such a luxury along) and gently lift the tail, as described earlier, to remove skin, rib cage and backbone. Liberally spread with butter and use more pieces of greaseproof paper for personal plates. This recipe is usually improved with the addition of a few cans of cold 'lemonade'.

STEAMED AND BAKED TROUT

This method is the outdoor equivalent of steaming a trout in the oven at home. It is very easy to do, and has given me many grand meals at campfires and in cabins throughout the back country of New Zealand, more especially in my safari days when I regularly cooked trout this way for my clients. All you need is salt, butter, a couple of medium onions and a complete local newspaper. Build up a good fire until you have a good hot bed of coals, and while this is building you can be preparing the trout. Into the stomach cavity place the sliced onions, some salt and a slice or two of butter, although on many occasions I have used nothing inside the trout. Cut the head off but leave the tail on. Wrap the trout tightly in the newspaper until you have an airtight parcel; it helps to tie it with string or twine to keep it from unwrapping. Place the parcel into a creek or lake until it is well soaked and then put it into a hole scraped in the hot coals and scrape coals over it until completely covered. You can now sit back for fifteen minutes which is as long as it takes to cook, and enjoy a lemonade or two while you are waiting. If you are not sure, give it another five minutes, but if you have a good bed of coals, twenty minutes will be all the time you will need. Scrape the charred parcel from the ashes and cut it open lengthwise with a knife—it is seldom possible to unwrap it. When the trout is exposed, you will be able to lift the tail to remove backbone and skin as above, and cover the flesh with butter. I don't have to tell you what to do with it then.

It is doubtful whether the two above methods can be improved on. They are tried and proven methods, although by all means experiment with sauces of various kinds. But it is the simplicity, enhanced by good company, a drop or two of the 'doings', and the never-ending stories of the big one that got away, that makes this type of outdoor cooking such a success.

SMOKED TROUT—COOKING METHOD

For a quick delicious lunch of trout, there is no better way than smoke-cooking them in a portable Kilwell smoker. This is a device marketed by most New Zealand sports stores in various sizes. The smallest takes up little room in the boot of a car or the bow of a boat, and to my mind is one of the finest fishing companions ever invented. With it, one can cook-smoke trout in ten to fifteen minutes and it can safely be used on the stern or bow of a boat or on shore without fear of causing a scrub or grass fire in the dry season. It is a favourite with top fishing guides because, even in a boat, one can carry on fishing while

189

lunch is cooking, which makes it a time-saver when clients are paying for fishing time. All you need to bring along is a bottle of methylated spirits for fuel, a small plastic bag of manuka sawdust, a roll of greaseproof paper, salt and pepper and butter.

First clean and fillet your trout and cut into small portions, leaving the skin on, as this helps hold the fillets together during cooking. The cooker comes apart and makes two separate boxes, the oven on top and the stove underneath. In the oven is a rack on which the fish fillets are laid, while sawdust is sprinkled on the floor of the oven beneath the fish and the lid is slid on. The stove portion has a container like a deep saucer, which is filled with methylated spirits. Light the spirits with a match and in minutes a smoky aroma will pervade the atmosphere, which is guaranteed to give any angler present—and all those within 100 metres—an instant appetite. Snuff the spirits out after 15 minutes and slide the lid off. The fillets can be lifted out with a knife or fork and placed on pieces of greaseproof paper. Cover them with butter, pepper and salt, and you are in for one of the tastiest meals you have ever had outdoors.

I have used a Kilwell out at sea for fish such as kahawai with equal success, and one of my friends uses his for guest suppers at home. When he runs out of trout, he cooks sausages and steaks in it.

SMOKING TROUT

Inevitably in every angler's experience comes the day when he catches a limit bag. He arrives home with a bulging bag of trout, slightly bewildered as to what he is going to do with them. Should thoughts then arise of wanting to preserve a few, by far the tastiest method of doing so is to smoke them. You can even build your own smoker, which is not as difficult an operation as one might think. Anyway, building instructions are included later (see page 192) for those who might want to take up this productive hobby either on a temporary or permanent basis.

Smoking trout—indeed, fish smoking in general—has its addicts and they are as many and varied as home brewers. Like them, each devotee claims to have the best method. For convenience, therefore, I will deal with the two most popular methods of smoking fish which are not too complicated.

The smoking procedure already described, using a Kilwell smoker, is known as the 'hot' method and is designed to cook the fish but not preserve it. The following methods, used in various ways by commercial smoke houses, are known as the 'cold' method and are designed to preserve as well as cook. They cure and preserve the flesh, with salt or brine as the preserving agent and the smoke acting as the drying agent as well as adding flavour and colour.

Preparation. When cleaning the trout, cut the head off but leave the skin and tail on. It also helps to leave the pectoral fins intact as they assist in laying the fish out flat on the drying racks or in pinning them if they are to be hung, as I shall explain later. Also cut into the backbone from inside the trout for its full length, so that you can lay the fish out flat like an open book. Always wipe all moisture from the flesh with a clean cloth.

COLD SMOKING—DRY SALT METHOD

After preparation, lay salt heavily on the flesh side of the trout and stack them flesh side to flesh side in a cardboard box or other container and leave them in this overnight. In the morning they can be rinsed in water to remove excess salt, dried off with a cloth and hung in the shade to dry. If you have the time, the above simple operation can be improved by first soaking the fish in a mixture of salt and water for an hour or so before drying off and placing in the box with salt. For drying, they should be hung in the shade, preferably in a safe, where the breeze can circulate for several hours, depending on air temperature, until a thin skin has formed on the flesh side. Just make sure there is no moisture on the trout before placing them in the smoke box (see below).

Brine method. A brine can be made up of equal quantities of salt and brown sugar, say 0.5 kg (1 lb approx.), added to a container of water. You can vary the amount of sugar, using a little less if the finished product is too sweet for your taste. To the brine, add one teaspoon of saltpetre. Have enough brine to make sure all the fish are well covered and leave them in it. Then dry the same as for the above method.

SMOKING

Leaving the pectoral fins on the trout adds a little weight, which helps to prevent the fish from curling during drying and smoking. They also give anchor points for the skewers which are necessary to help keep the fish flat if laid on racks or as something to hook on to if hung in the smokehouse (Fig. 7). Skewers can be made from number eight wire or green sticks and should be pointed on one end so that they can be laced across the fish from pectoral fin to pectoral fin. It is best to place the skewers when the trout are hung out to dry.

Manuka sawdust makes the best fuel. It is durable, hot and fragrant. The smoke and heat reaching the fish should be neither too

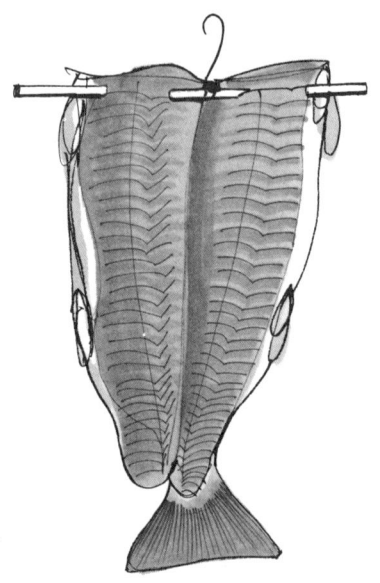

Figure 7. How to insert skewer to lay fish out flat for smoking. Skewered fish can be hung from hook (illustrated) or laid on wire mesh.

plentiful nor too hot, a desirable temperature around the fish being about 25°C. If this temperature is kept up for 8–12 hours, the trout should keep for a week or more and longer if placed in a fridge. The time and temperature depend on the thoroughness of the operator and experimentation will eventually give you a tried and proven method. The main point to remember in smoking fish is that you will need less smoke and heat than you think necessary, so a little less of both over a longer period will turn out the best product. During smoking, test a fish occasionally after several hours to see how the processing is coming along.

BUILDING A SMOKER

New Zealanders are famous for their adaptability and ingenuity— good old Kiwi 'know how'—and around the lakes and streams you will find smokers or their remains in all sorts of odd places. Which goes to prove that if you are camped out for a few days and getting good bags, it is not too hard to rig up a temporary smoker to preserve your catch. A temporary smoker can be built out of almost anything at hand—bushy manuka branches, scrim, an old piece of canvas or polythene (Fig. 8). The chosen material can be built up or laced around several green poles, wigwam style, with a green sapling pushed across half way up like a perch in a budgie cage to hang the

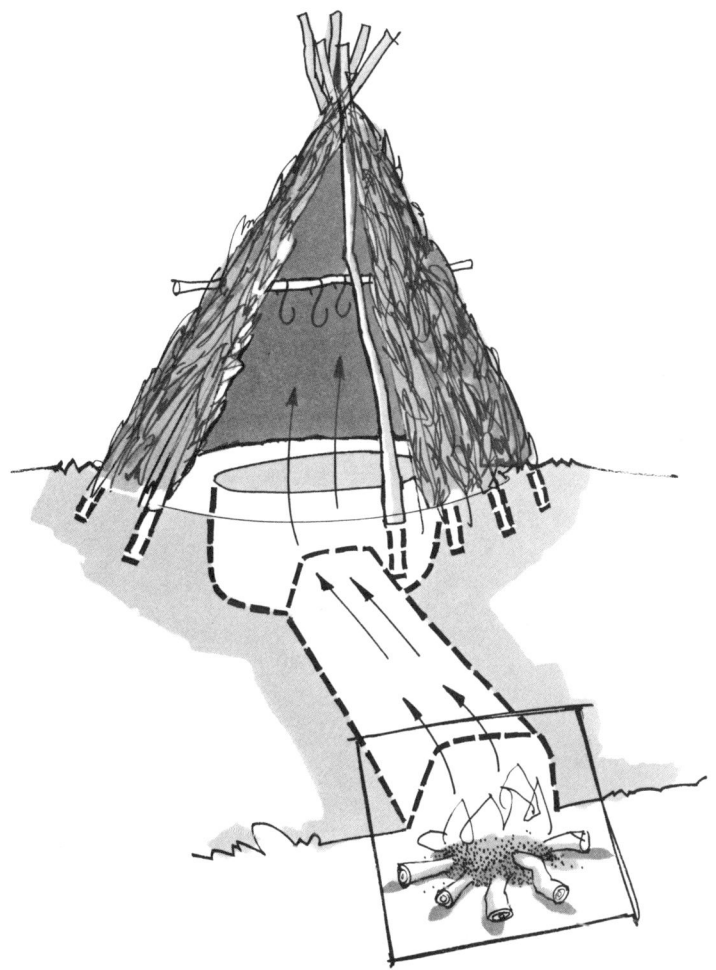

Figure 8. Makeshift temporary smoker built on camp location from materials at hand such as manuka scrub and poles.

fish from. Laced manuka branches will give ample vents for the smoke to escape but in using scrim, canvas or polythene, holes will need to be cut with a knife near the top for this purpose.

The fire should be built on a level with or slightly below the base of the smoker and at least a metre away from it. In other words, the smoke from the fire should travel through a tunnel to the base of the smoker, thus giving the smoke a little time to cool. The tunnel can be dug with a spade, lifting the sods more or less whole and supporting them on crossed sticks to form the top, or a cover can be made, say, from a sheet of old iron. I have seen all sorts of makeshift tunnels and there is plenty of scope for ingenuity in this department.

193

Figure 9. Backyard smoker made from standard 200 litre (44 gallon) drum.

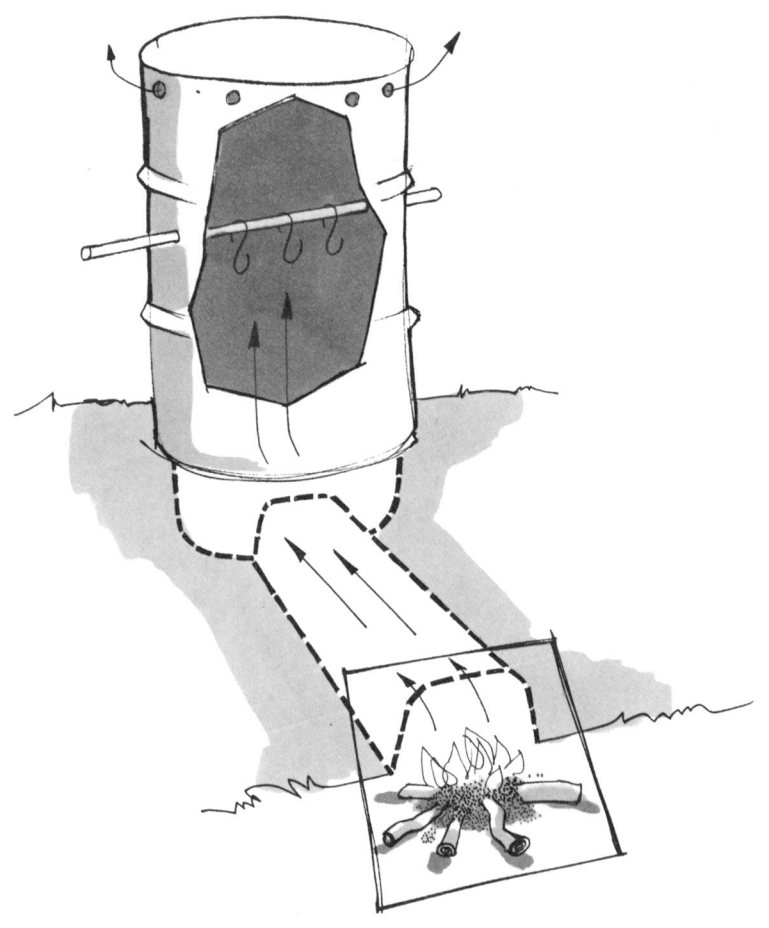

At home you can build a more permanent structure or do what most people do and adapt a standard steel drum for the purpose (Fig. 9). With both ends cut out, the drum is stood upright, possibly over a shallow depression along which the tunnel can lead in from the fire, the tunnel being dug as described above or made from a tube of galvanised iron. A lid can be made from wood or the drum end to allow access and holes are punctured around the top of the drum just under the lid to let the smoke out. These holes can be plugged or unplugged as need be to help control the draught. Tightly fitting steel rods—as tight a fit as possible—are poked through from side to side of the drum for fish racks.

Alternative smokers can be constructed all of wood (Fig. 10) or perhaps adapted from an old refrigerator, which at least would have a ready-made door. Like an old wine barrel, any smoker will improve with maturity.

To light the sawdust, first get a good fire going with dry wood then add the sawdust to the glowing embers, taking care not to smother the fire. To prevent smothering, I would suggest making an opening in the fire by placing two short thickish logs side by side across the embers a few centimetres apart. They will let air in under the sawdust and prevent it going out. As the fire is built at the tunnel entrance, it will be necessary to cover it with a sheet of metal to make sure the smoke goes up the tunnel. Care should be taken not to have too much draught up the tunnel to the fish, as the heat and smoke will then be too plentiful. As already mentioned, the draught can be controlled by blocking or unblocking the holes at the top of the smoker.

The satisfaction an angler receives from a well turned out product should not be lost sight of. It gives him a chance to prove that everyone can enjoy the end product as much as he did catching it. Frankly I could not tell you how long a trout will keep once it has been smoked. They never last long enough in our house to find out.

A final word of caution. Remember it is an offence to leave unburied fish cleanings and rubbish around fishing spots. If you cannot bury bulky rubbish such as bottles and cans, bring them home with you.

Figure 10. Suggested layout for a permanent wooden smoker easily built by a handyman.

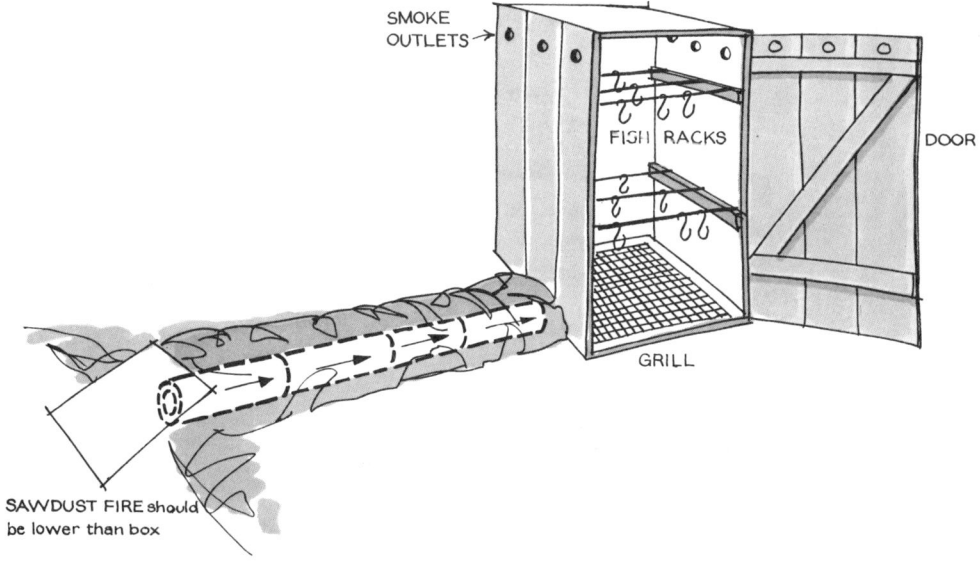

SMOKE OUTLETS

FISH RACKS

DOOR

GRILL

SAWDUST FIRE should be lower than box

New Zealand Angling Regulations

Wildlife Service ranger Harry Tanfield, having arrived by jetboat, checks out the bag of some visiting anglers under the watchful eye of fishing guide Bill Hogan. River is the Hunter, top dry-fly water, which flows into Lake Hawea, West Otago

As shown on the accompanying North Island and South Island maps (pages 202, 203), there are at present twenty-three acclimatisation societies controlling fishing in different districts of New Zealand. In addition the Department of Internal Affairs administers two large acclimatisation districts, one in each island, the Rotorua district in the north (which includes the Taupo fishing district) and the Southern Lakes district in the south. The maps merely outline the general areas, though some necessary boundary rivers and natural features are also named.

All twenty-three acclimatisation societies issue whole-season fishing licences which may be used to take acclimatised fish in each and every one of these districts. The societies also issue short-term and single-water licences. A short-term licence (half season, month,

week or day) may be used only within the district of issue, while a single-water licence may be used only for a certain named water in the district of issue.

Whole-season licences as above cannot be used in the districts administered by the Department of Internal Affairs, for which separate licences are required. Indeed, separate licences are issued for the three districts, Rotorua, Taupo and Southern Lakes, even though the Taupo fishing district is included in the Rotorua acclimatisation district. Special restrictions applying to these licences are:

(a) Any Taupo fishing licence may be used in the Taupo fishing district and on the Waikato River down to the Waimahana bridge at Mihi only.

(b) Any Rotorua fishing licence may be used elsewhere within the Rotorua acclimatisation district (but not in the Taupo fishing district) and on the Waikato River up to the Huka Falls.

A Southern Lakes fishing licence is restricted to use within that acclimatisation district. Regulations for these three districts can be purchased for a small fee from the Wildlife Service, Internal Affairs Department, Private Bag, Wellington.

General fishing regulations and those governing special district requirements are usually printed on the back of the fishing licence. It is worth noting that most acclimatisation societies have different regulations governing open seasons, limit bags and length of fish which can be taken. Where a licence is being lawfully used in another acclimatisation district than the district of issue, the local restrictions of the district being fished apply.

The following general regulations and restrictions apply to all fishing districts in New Zealand. They are listed under different heads simply for the convenience of the reader and do not carry any official 'weight' in this summary form.

GENERAL

1. The open season is usually 1 October to 30 April of the following year.
2. A person is regarded as fishing at the place from where he is fishing and at the place to which his lure reaches.
3. Acclimatised fish include trout, salmon, char, perch and tench.

FISHING LICENCES

4. No licence is transferable.

5. No licence is valid until signed by the licensee.
6. The licence must be carried when fishing, produced when requested by an authorised person, and a specimen signature must be given when required by an authorised officer.

FISHING TACKLE

7. Angling outfit, bag, all baits, etc., in possession must be shown on request to an authorised officer.
8. Angling is permitted with one rod and running line only. Landing net and gaff are permitted unless forbidden by special district regulations.
9. Rod must be held or be in sight and within 15 metres (50 ft) of the angler (except Rotorua, Taupo and Southern Lakes).
10. Only one assembled outfit may be used at a time.
11. Hand lines, stroke-hauling gear, paravanes, otters, firearms, explosives, poisons, spears, nets and other unsportsmanlike gear are prohibited.
12. Chemical preparations except dry-fly oil and natural bait preservatives are illegal.
13. Lead, loaded lures and lead-cored wire are illegal in fly waters.
14. Unless expressly permitted by special district regulations, the following are illegal:
    (a) One-piece rods of over 3.4 metres (11 ft) —except Rotorua, Taupo and Southern Lakes.
    (b) More than two lures or baits.
    (c) More than one hook with artificial fly.
    (d) Wire traces of over 1.8 metres (6 ft) or heavier than 21-gauge.
    (e) With spoon bait or artificial minnow, any weight or lead fixed to the trace or line at a distance of less than 38 cm (15 in) above the lure.
    (f) With spoon bait, minnow or other lure, any treble hook, any one hook which has a gape greater than 12 mm ($\frac{1}{2}$ in).
    (g) Any lead or weight attached below any lure or bait.

SIZE AND BAGS

15. Limit bag is the maximum number of fish that can be kept by one person within a 24-hour period from midnight.
16. Size limit is the minimum size of the fish which may be lawfully taken, measured from the tip of the nose to the tip of the tail.

NOTE: (a) There is no size or bag limit for perch unless mentioned in district regulations.

(b) Undersized fish must be returned to the water unharmed.

LURES AND BAITS

17. Lawful baits include the following unless prohibited by district regulations: Artificial or natural fly, minnow, spoon, insect, worm, crustacea or fish.

NOTE: All other lures such as bread, curd, ova, shellfish, meat, etc., are illegal. Most districts have some specially restricted waters.

18. Artificial fly includes any lure or feather, fur, wool or similar material in which no lead or other weight has been incorporated to facilitate casting or sinking, though some districts allow weighted nymphs.

19. Artificial minnow includes spoon bait, any feather lure in which lead or other weight has been incorporated to facilitate casting or sinking of the lure, and any lure which incorporates a spinning device or devices to impart a wobbling or irregular motion.

SELLING AND CANNING

20. Trout or salmon must not be sold.
21. Canned trout restrictions:
    (a) A limit of 25 kg (55 lb) in possession of one person.
    (b) Angler's name, licence number, date and place of capture to be engraved or painted in oil paint on each can immediately.
    (c) Disposal of unmarked cans is illegal.
    (d) Angling while in possession of unmarked cans is illegal.

SMOKE HOUSES

22. A register of fish being smoked must be kept and made available for inspection.
23. Each type of fish must be correctly identified.
24. Smoke house charges cannot be paid for with trout.

MISCELLANEOUS

25. Offal and cleanings from fish dressed at the water's edge must be buried.
26. Capture of marked or tagged fish must be notified to the local

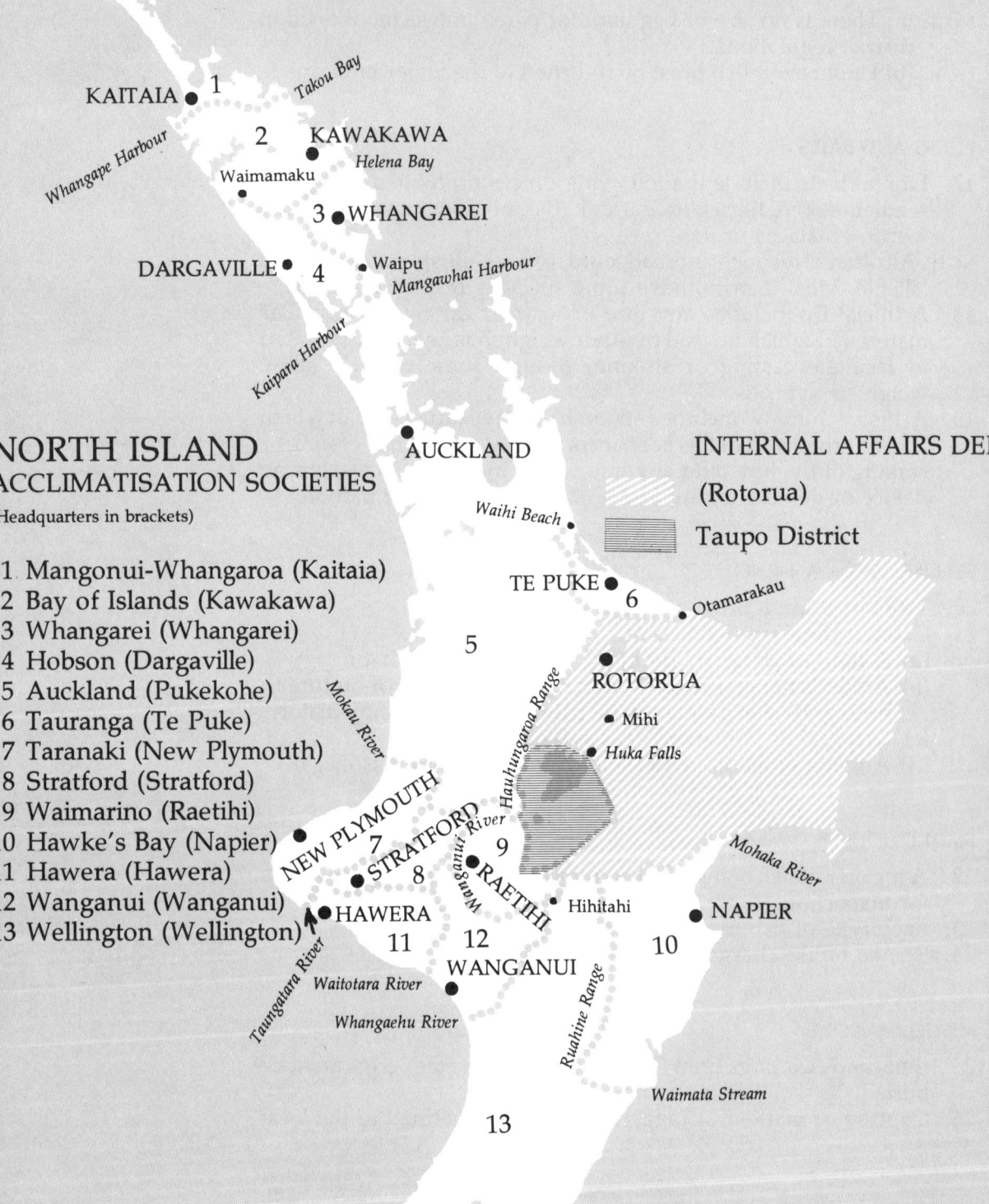

KAITAIA ● 1
Takou Bay
2 ● KAWAKAWA
Whangape Harbour
Helena Bay
Waimamaku ●
3 ● WHANGAREI
DARGAVILLE ● 4
Waipu ●
Mangawhai Harbour
Kaipara Harbour

AUCKLAND ●

NORTH ISLAND
ACCLIMATISATION SOCIETIES
(Headquarters in brackets)

1 Mangonui-Whangaroa (Kaitaia)
2 Bay of Islands (Kawakawa)
3 Whangarei (Whangarei)
4 Hobson (Dargaville)
5 Auckland (Pukekohe)
6 Tauranga (Te Puke)
7 Taranaki (New Plymouth)
8 Stratford (Stratford)
9 Waimarino (Raetihi)
10 Hawke's Bay (Napier)
11 Hawera (Hawera)
12 Wanganui (Wanganui)
13 Wellington (Wellington)

INTERNAL AFFAIRS DEP

(Rotorua)

Taupo District

Waihi Beach ●

TE PUKE ● 6
Otamarakau ●

5

ROTORUA

Mokau River

● Mihi

Huka Falls ●

Hauhungaroa Range

NEW PLYMOUTH 7
STRATFORD
8
Wanganui River
9
RAETIHI
Hihitahi ●

Mohaka River

HAWERA
11 12
WANGANUI
NAPIER ●
10

Taungatara River
Waitotara River
Whangaehu River

Ruahine Range

Waimata Stream

13

WELLINGTON ●

SOUTH ISLAND
ACCLIMATISATION SOCIETIES
(Headquarters in brackets)

14 Nelson (Nelson)
15 Marlborough (Blenheim)
16 West Coast (Greymouth)
17 North Canterbury (Christchurch)
18 Westland (Hokitika)
19 Ashburton (Ashburton)
20 South Canterbury (Timaru)
21 Waitaki Valley (Oamaru)
22 Otago (Dunedin)
23 Southland (Invercargill)

INTERNAL AFFAIRS DEPT
Southern Lakes

Kohaihai River

LYELL RANGE

NELSON

ST ARNAUD RANGE

BLENHEIM

14

15

Conway River

16

GREYMOUTH

Taramakau Rv

HOKITIKA

ALPS

17

18

SOUTHERN

Rakaia River

Makawhio Point

19

Rangitata River

ASHBURTON

CHRISTCHURCH

20

TIMARU

Pareora River

21

QUEENSTOWN

GARVIE MOUNTAINS

KAKANUI MOUNTAINS

OAMARU

Shag Point

22

DUNEDIN

23

Mataura River

Te Waewae Bay
INVERCARGILL

acclimatisation society or district office of the Department of Internal Affairs. Unauthorised marking or tagging is illegal.

27. Release of fish or any form of life in any water is illegal without special authority. NOTE: Does not include releasing fish into waters from which they were taken.

QUINNAT SALMON

28. Between 1 January and 30 April, when fishing for trout or salmon in a river containing quinnat salmon (except the Clutha River), use artificial minnow with one assembly of hooks, gape not to exceed 12 mm (½ in) and lead to be not less than 38 cm (15 in).

The above are the main regulations applying to all districts and acclimatisation societies. It is necessary to stress again, however, that each district and society has its own additional regulations applying to that district covering seasons, limit bags, restricted areas and so on. It is recommended that every angler fishing in a strange district check these local regulations for his own protection.

Author plays a leaping rainbow on the Whakapapa River just west of Mount Ruapehu

ILLUSTRATION ACKNOWLEDGMENTS

Many photographs have been taken by the author. Those gratefully acknowledged to other photographers and sources appear on the following pages:
National Publicity Studios, 3-4, 9, 13, 43, 63, 81, 87, 124, 131, 132 135, 138, 146–7, 155, 156, 159, 160, 174, 184, 198, 205
Norrie Ewing, 17, 18
Daily Post, Rotorua, 20, 33
Mrs Charles Waterman, De Land, Florida, 74
Courtesy Mrs Rea Potts, 80
Courtesy Fred Gill, 88
Martin Barraball, 91
Hazeldine Studios, Invercargill, 165
John Gates drew the illustrations in Chapter 11
Simon Dickie, 48
House of Maxwell, Taupo, 67
Gary Kemsley, 88